Satisfied is an invitation to be free ... to shake off the stuff that smothers us and live like the lilies and the sparrows. A thoughtful reminder to share the stuff we own before it owns us, and to get money out of our hands before it makes its way into our hearts. It is a call to laugh at the lie of our culture that tells us happiness has a price tag.

> —SHANE CLAIBORNE, author, activist, and recovering
> consumer *www.thesimpleway.org*

Jeff Manion's voice is such a wise, clear, helpful voice, and I'm so thankful for the timely and challenging invitation he has issued in these pages. I'm inspired to live more richly with fewer things, and to pursue gratitude and generosity with more intention.

> —SHAUNA NIEQUIST, author of *Bread & Wine*

Some books can be skimmed, others read, and some should be chewed on slowly and digested fully. This book falls into the third category. As you savor this book, God will speak deeply and transform your life in surprising ways.

> —REV. KEVIN G. HARNEY (www.kevingharney.com),
> lead pastor of Shoreline Church in Monterey, CA, and
> author of *Reckless Faith* and the *Organic Outreach* Series.

Comparison kills contentment. But when is enough, enough? In *Satisfied*, Jeff Manion shows how having less is a gift that leads to freedom.

> —BOB MERRITT, pastor of Eagle Brook Church in
> St. Paul, MN, and author of *When Life's Not Working*

My friend Jeff Manion is offering *Satisfied* to everyone who struggles with the angst of joy. As joy gushes, they wonder at their ongoing discontent. "Is it OK to be happy if others aren't? Should I get used to this? Will I lose this joy if I share it? How do I find more of this; does it come from what happens 'in' me, or 'to' me?" Manion's winsome style makes *Satisfied* more than a great read and a phenomenal Small Group resource; it helps people take steps into a satisfied and joy-filled life.

> —DR. MARK BEESON, founding pastor of Granger
> Community Church in Granger, IN

Being satisfied seems more like a process than a result—this book is a great tool for the process!

> —BRAD FORMSMA, creator of *www.Ilikegiving.com*
> and author of *I like Giving*

In a debt-ridden and consumer driven society, few people are experiencing true contentment, freedom, and joy in their financial lives. Jeff Manion's outstanding book *Satified* will help you learn how to do just that. It offers engaging and practical insights that are life changing because they are based on God's word. I heartily recommend it!

> —HOWARD DAYTON, founder, Compass—*finances
> God's way*

Jeff is a master storyteller, and you will see yourself on every page. Get *Satisfied* and get contentment, God's way!

> —CLARE DE GRAAF, author of *The 10-Second Rule*

Satisfied

See the author's webpage at: jeffmanion.org.

Twitter: manionjeff

Satisfied

Discovering Contentment
in a World of Consumption

JEFF MANION

ZONDERVAN

Satisfied
Copyright © 2013 by Jeff Manion

This title is also available as a Zondervan ebook. Visit www.zondervan.com/ebooks.

Requests for information should be addressed to:

Zondervan, *Grand Rapids, Michigan* 49530

Library of Congress Cataloging-in-Publication Data

Manion, Jeff, 1962 –
    Satisfied / Jeff Manion
         p. cm.
      Includes bibliographical references and index
      ISBN 978-0-310-32835-3 (softcover)
        1. Contentment – Religious aspects – Christianity. 2. Satisfaction – Religious aspects – Christianity. 3. Consumption (Economics) – Religious aspects – Christianity. I. Title.
    BV4647.C7M365   2014
    241'.68 – dc23   2013026571

Cover design: Dual Identity
Cover photography: Shutterstock®
Interior illustration: Part art, Beth Shagene
Interior design: Beth Shagene

Printed in the United States of America

---

13 14 15 16 17 18 19 /DCI/ 22 21 20 19 18 17 16 15 14 13 12 11 10 9 8 7 6 5 4 3 2 1

Contents

In Search of the Satisfied Life

In his classic monologue, comedian George Carlin riffed on the mountain of stuff we compile. His assertion is that "a house is just a pile of stuff with a cover on it."

> So when you get right down to it, your house is nothing more than a place to keep your stuff ... while you go out and get ... more stuff. 'Cause that's what this country is all about. Trying to get more stuff. Stuff you don't want, stuff you don't need, stuff that's poorly made, stuff that's overpriced. Even stuff you can't afford! Gotta keep on getting more stuff.
>
> So you keep gettin' more and more stuff, and puttin' it in different places. In the closets, in the attic, in the basement, in the garage.... So now you got a houseful of stuff. And, even though you might like your house, you gotta move. Gotta get a bigger house. Why? Too much stuff!
>
> *Brain Droppings*, 37, 38

Carlin's social commentary, cloaked in comedic humor, hits close to home. The piece connects with audiences so well because we detect the reality that lies behind the laughter. We are addicted to amassing stuff.

Awakening

If we are fortunate, we awaken to our surplus. While on a brief trip to a children's hospital in the Dominican Republic, a woman visits a family whose child will soon undergo surgery. Their cinderblock house is windowless. Six people reside in the space roughly the size of a one-stall garage. An ensemble of plastic molded chairs comprises the furniture. Then there is the flight home and reentrance to her own world and house — the house she felt was simple and modest just eight days before. Suddenly she awakens to the opulence of her "simplicity." The trip does not induce guilt as much as offer a healthy reality check.

Excursions like this provide the opportunity to recast our categories for wealth, simplicity, and shortage. A door is opened, allowing us to see our stuff in a new light and to wonder what motivations drive us to amass the things that pile up around us.

Rethinking

Then we encounter the teachings of Jesus—his rather straightforward comments directed at our propensity to define our lives by what we own.

"Life does not consist in an abundance of possessions."

"Where your treasure is, there your heart will be also."

"You cannot serve both God and money."

"Watch out! Be on your guard against all kinds of greed."

"I have come that they may have life, and have it to the full."

I find his words piercing. As a professing Christian, I have the responsibility to consider my buying habits, not simply as a middle-class American, but as a Jesus follower. Personally, I feel stalked by some pretty convicting questions. As one who allegedly follows the Christ, what claims does Jesus have on my wallet? What does it mean to think Christianly about the stuff that fills my closet, garage, and basement? How does the one I call "Lord" intend to reshape my attitudes toward spending, accumulating, and giving?

My suspicion is that we have simply lost our way. I suspect that our material longings are more largely formed by our culture than by the Christ and that our spending habits do not differ radically from those who have no allegiance or loyalty to Jesus.

It might be helpful if we begin our journey with a mutual confession: We live in a consumer-driven, debt-ridden, advertisement-saturated culture, and it will require nothing short of total transformation to adopt the heart and brain of Jesus. The current in which we swim is so strong that it will take immense focus and intentionality to keep us from being swept downstream and ultimately pulled under. Make no mistake about it: if you determine to seek the satisfied, contented life, you will be swimming against the current.

The First Christians

The challenges faced by early Christians were not that different from our own. This first generation of believers who populated cities of Ephesus, Laodicea, and Corinth also wrestled with insidious materialism. By traveling back to their world, we will gain insight into following Jesus in ours. Together we will explore the encouragement given to these first believers as they were coached to find financial sanity through Christ's sufficiency. *Satisfied* will draw deeply from six passages of Scripture, discovering the way these messages were received by the original readers, and the way these passages can transform how we view our stuff.

The goal is to provide biblical direction for living a deep spiritual life in a shallow, materialistic culture. Together we will explore our insatiable hunger for material possessions and journey toward the countercultural lifestyle of contented satisfaction.

At the end of each part you will find thought-provoking questions and challenging projects. These are vital if the information in these chapters is to take root and lead to life transformation. The projects, in particular, have the potential of realigning our behavior—translating information into action. Take the time to thoughtfully reflect on these questions and diligently pursue the projects. I think you will find them engaging and eye-opening, and hopefully they will be the first steps toward your satisfied life.

This Book Is for You

- I have written *Satisfied* for those drowning in debt—but also for those getting farther and farther ahead who desire a legacy more compelling than obsessive accumulation.

- I write these words for those crippled by comparison—whose frame of reference is shaped by what they lack rather than the blessings they possess. Comparison is a thief, stealing gratitude, joy, and generosity.

- *Satisfied* is for those who have forgotten who they are and mistakenly equate their self- worth with their net worth.

- These words are for you if your salary is growing but your generosity isn't. If you find yourself shopping when you are lonely, bored, or depressed, these thoughts were penned with you in mind. It is for those with full closets and empty souls.

- I write this book for those who desire to think "Christianly" about what we have and what we crave. It is for thoughtful believers desiring to think more biblically about our stuff. It is also for those outside the Christian faith who desire perspective on how the Bible speaks into the topics of contentment and accumulation.

I invite you to join me in the journey of discovering the satisfied life.

PART 1

The School of Contentment

01

Material World

Stuff

Members of the Natomo family sit on the flat roof of their mud house in Mali, Africa, posing for the early morning photograph. Their earthly belongings are arrayed in front of them. Two kettles, plastic water containers, woven baskets, an assortment of agricultural tools, and a fishing net can be identified among the objects. Their village has no electricity, paved roads, or cars, but a battery-operated radio sits at the father's feet, and behind him on the roof is his transportation: a bicycle. The overall impression is scarcity—simplicity driven by shortage.

The portrait of the Wu family from China differs significantly as seven members of the extended family stare into the camera from their perches in a long, narrow boat that floats on the fish pond beside their home. The two adult sons, adorned in hip waders, stand in the shallow water at opposite ends of their vessel. A coffee table sits in the middle of the bobbing boat, a TV precariously balanced upon it. Other household possessions are staged on shore in front of the Wus's home—bicycles, electric fans, a guitar, clothing, a sewing machine, a rice cooker, a table, a sofa, and dinnerware. The image evokes the impression of moderate prosperity achieved through diligence and industry.

I first encountered these captivating portraits while waiting for an international flight in Chicago. The art exhibit featured families from around the world, sitting in front of their homes, surrounded by their possessions. The pictures were part of a project envisioned by photojournalist Peter Menzel, who desired to capture the lifestyles of average families around the globe. His book *Material World* leads us on a photographic journey into the lives and possessions of families from thirty different countries.

From time to time I thumb through my copy of Menzel's book, fascinated when I think about the stuff we surround ourselves with. Some items are objects of daily use—microwave, coffeemaker, bed, boots. Others are keepsakes that hold sentimental value for one reason or another—family pictures, high school yearbooks, sets of dishes passed down from our grandmothers. But other belongings are neither cherished nor used. You know, the stuff that we bought once upon a time that just sort of sits there, or hangs there, or is piled there—clothing no longer worn, books never read, shoes that haven't seen daylight in years, dusty exercise equipment purchased with lofty intentions.

My suspicion is that, most often, we are unconscious and unreflective of the mass of stuff we somehow managed to accumulate. Then comes a moment of clarity, say moving day, when we are faced with physically lifting and packing hundreds — thousands — of items. Suddenly we come in tactile contact with the sum of our acquisitions. Hours of handling, lifting, sorting, and boxing can prompt a couple to question, "Where did we get all this crap?"

My friend Brian experienced this sensation after a fire left his spacious home in ruins. He sifted through the remnants, cataloging and bagging every item for accurate reporting to the insurance company. Itemizing each and every shirt and shoe, pot and pan, book and blender was a staggering experience for him. I suspect these moments when we are assaulted by the sum of our gathered goods are exceedingly rare. It usually does take an arriving moving van or a departing fire truck to truly reckon with the mountain of possessions we surround ourselves with.

Lightening the Load

Recently I was exposed to my own world of accumulation when I embarked on a project to give things away. Namely, my goal was to rid my life of five items a day for six weeks. That amounted to thirty-five objects a week, a total of 210 items over the six-week experiment — which was prompted by reading Jen Hatmaker's book, *7: An Experimental Mutiny Against Excess*.

At the outset, I need to emphasize that this project was not an exercise in generosity. To be truly generous, a gift should probably cost you something, and most of the items I relinquished were belongings I never used and wouldn't miss. This was more a mission to de-clutter—a modest attempt to rid my life of some excess baggage. But I found the six-week exercise immensely helpful in identifying previously undetected patterns of acquiring and accumulating. Before I chronicle the six weeks, I need to mention that my wife, Chris, faithfully rids our home of outdated, unworn, and unused stuff. We are not pack rats, and we have a general allergy to clutter. I have no hoarding instincts … or so I thought.

Week 1

I venture to the basement and exhume a box of VHS tapes—thirty-five of them in all, coincidently matching the number of items I desire to rid my life of for Week 1. I say good-bye to the Star Wars Trilogy, *Little Rascals*, *Mission Impossible*, a boxed set of National Geographic videos, and so on. We no longer have a VHS player, haven't had one for years, yet the tapes have hibernated in a box in the basement storage room. They are now obsolete to our lives. I cart them off to a thrift store that still sells VHS tapes. As I said, this is not generosity, just cleansing.

Week 2

In the kitchen, Chris removes a dish set from a cupboard. Forty pieces in all—large plates, small plates, serving bowl, and mugs. The set is beautiful. We simply never use it. I'm guessing it's been two years since these dishes have shared our table. They nestle in the cupboard, attractive and unused. Chris donates these to Safe Haven Ministries, a nonprofit in our area that provides transitional housing. This donation feels more heartfelt than the VHS tapes I jettisoned last week. We genuinely hope that the meals of a temporarily displaced family will be enriched because of the dinnerware.

Week 3

I cart off a box with three dozen CDs. Unlike owning VHS tapes with no VHS player, we do still have a CD player, but we use it decreasingly. The music that floods our home generally emits from computer and iPod rather than from our shuffling CDs. I found the CDs sleeping in the same basement storage room that dormed our VHS tapes. I haul them to the same thrift store.

Week 4

I sift through my clothing, filling a large box with items I never wear or simply don't need. Among the items are shoes, shorts, hats, and coats—but mostly shirts. I have no conscious recollection of making it my ambition to amass printed T-shirts, but they seem to multiply. They follow me home from 5K races, conferences, and events. I frequently wear T-shirts, but I feel I have collected enough to outfit a small village.

And the shoes. I toss nine pair, and I'm not a shoe guy! I don't accessorize. I wear the same boring pair of black dress shoes to church every weekend. But between running, hiking and biking, dress and casual, formal and flip-flops—the shoes have compounded. What I discovered were shoes I'd worn out, yet had not discarded. I wear through a couple of pairs of running shoes a year, yet fail to toss the old ones when I purchase new ones. In the shoe bins, I discover three pairs of old running shoes. Clutter. Out they go. Ditto with biking shoes that have faithfully lived out their effective lifespan and a pair of flip-flops that do nothing but take up space. As I scan my closet, I'm also reintroduced to a pair of brown dress shoes that I haven't worn in at least three years—and am unlikely to don in the next three. I reduce my stockpile, but this reduction is un-heroic. I will not miss any of these things. They are simply excess baggage.

Week 5

Week 5 comes after the Christmas holidays. In addition to our gathering a pile of old Christmas CDs and a moderate stack of books from my library, Chris culls an assortment of

Christmas objects — think here of hot-chocolate-Santa-mug-type items. All of these will go to the same thrift store we have visited in recent weeks.

But among the discarded items is one object I trust will have a good home: a new, expensive, unopened, leather-bound study Bible that I received as a gift but has been sitting on a shelf, still sheathed in its original box. Apparently, the rightful owner of this sacred volume is not me. I transfer custody of the Bible to a dear friend, whom I suspect might love and use it.

Week 6

In my final week, it's time to hit the garage. Among the items evicted from my life are my older pair of cross-country skis, a tennis racket, a couple of random golf clubs, a thermos, extension cords, and a hockey stick. I have no idea why this hockey stick has collected dust in my garage for the past eight years — there is not a hockey player among us, unless my wife silently sneaks out to covertly play in a midnight league, for which I would give low odds.

Reflection

Six weeks, a couple hundred items, and a few insights gleaned from the experience.

Impression: Like emerging from a healthy weight-loss

program, I feel 210 items lighter. I feel freer. The reduction feels liberating. Ironically, I feel richer for owning less.

Impression: I'm jarred by the time gap that exists between obsolescence and cleansing. It appears that I stop using something long before I chuck it. If we moved to southern Florida, how long would I retain my snow shovel before confessing that perhaps we don't need one anymore?

Impression: I will not miss any of the belongings I carried from my home. If a burglar had stealthily entered our house and swiped these objects, weeks would have passed before their absence was detected.

Impression: I wonder how many more weeks of effort could remove thirty-five items from my house every seven days and still not dip into those objects that I really enjoy, use, or truly need. I have a feeling that simplicity is a long way off. Materially, I still feel heavy.

All this has me thinking about what we accumulate and why. In the midst of amassing far more than I need or could ever use, I'm unnerved by these convicting words on the contented life.

> But godliness with contentment is great gain. For we brought nothing into the world, and we can take nothing out of it. But if we have food and clothing, we will be content with that. (1 Timothy 6:6–8)

I suspect that most of us reading these sentences about

contentment could confess that we have drifted far from the mark. These powerful statements were penned by the apostle Paul to his protégé Timothy, while the younger pastor was leading the Jesus community in Ephesus. While we may concede that this guidance is highly relevant to our consumer-driven, commercial-saturated culture, it might come as a bit of a surprise that it was badly needed in the early church.

Shopping in Ephesus

I fell in love with maps as a child in church. The congregations my father pastored were small with no children's classes offered during the adult services. So I sat through his sermons, sometimes listening and sometimes killing time. Often I would open a Bible to the colorful maps in the back and trace ancient journeys across foreign landscapes and distant seas. The biblical cities of Ephesus, Corinth, Philippi, and Laodicea were merely dots on a map evoking nothing to distinguish these locations from one another. As a child sitting on a wooden pew and thumbing through the colorful pages as I waited for the sermon to end, I had no clue that I would one day be privileged to travel extensively to these sites.

Over the years, I have had the privilege of exploring Ephesus on a number of occasions. On my first visit I was stunned as I walked the wide marble streets, ascended the steps of the massive theater, and marveled at the opulence of the terrace houses. Suddenly Ephesus sprang to life, becoming a three-dimensional home to architects, builders, politicians, sailors, wholesalers, and retailers.

In the first century, Ephesus was the fourth most populous city in the Roman world, surpassed only by Rome, Alexandria, and Antioch in Syria. Ephesus dominated trade along the Aegean coastline. Its harbor hosted ships from throughout the Mediterranean, and roads connected the metropolis to

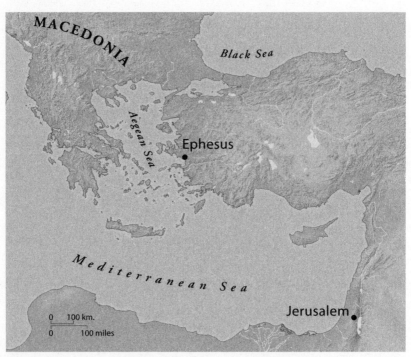

Ephesus in Asia Minor (Turkey).

manufacturing and agricultural centers to the East. The city had enormous wealth and a near endless variety of objects for people to acquire. In today's terms, Ephesus would compare to Hong Kong or New York.

Visit the ancient marketplace — or agora — of Ephesus with me. Just up the street from the sprawling, twenty-five-thousand-seat theater, we pass through an ornate, triple-arched gateway and enter the expansive retail space. (It's roughly the area of two football fields side by side.) A wide, covered walkway runs around the perimeter of the central, open-air courtyard, providing shade from the summer sun and protection from winter rains. The walkway connects the spacious courtyard in the middle with approximately a hundred shops that line the square. In this shopping area you can buy almost anything imaginable: the latest clothing fashions from Rome, Egyptian jewelry, purple cloth from Thyatira, or exotic spices from the East.

The agora of Ephesus was truly an international shopping center. I think a visit to this marketplace would feel similar to the congested pedestrian traffic I experience when walking the Magnificent Mile on Michigan Avenue in Chicago with its seemingly endless options in a long stretch of stores.

Timothy was serving in an epicenter of buying and selling, a hub of trade and commerce. The city had great wealth and no shortage of items to buy. From the standpoint of consumer opportunity, their world was not that different from ours. It is in this prosperous climate that Paul encouraged contentment. His words had huge relevance to that young pastor in Ephesus, but they can also profoundly affect our attitudes toward what we have, what we need, and what we want.

The Freedom of Contentment

Godliness with contentment is great gain.

(1 Timothy 6:6)

When Paul extolled the life of contentment, he was describing an inner fullness that was not contingent on material comfort. In his own case, he had experienced contentment even in highly uncomfortable conditions. A partial listing of what he encountered during his adventures includes shipwreck, flogging, mugging, treacherous river crossings, nights without sleep, and hunger (see 2 Corinthians 11:23–27), yet he was able to testify, "I have learned to be content whatever the circumstances" (Philippians 4:11).

Contentment is the cultivation of a satisfied heart. It is the discipline of being fully alive to God and to others whatever our material circumstances. Contentment is not achieved through getting everything we want but by training the heart to experience full joy and deep peace even when we don't have what we want.

Cradle to Grave

Even when we get what we desire, when we find something we really like and purchase it, we should be conscious that this new possession is only ours temporarily. I may think it is "mine," but it is really only "mine for now."

When Paul challenged Timothy to a lifestyle of contentment, he drew upon the logic of transience—not simply that our stuff will come and go but that *we* come and go. He reminds him, "For we brought nothing into this world, and we can take nothing out of it" (1 Timothy 6:7).

Paul was not the original biblical author of this proverb. It first comes to us from one of the earliest stories in the Bible—the story of Job, the man of great wealth who gets financially wrecked in a single day. When Job learns that he has lost everything, he exclaims, "Naked I came from my mother's womb, and naked I will depart. The LORD gave and the LORD has taken away; may the name of the LORD be praised" (1:21). Job's comment about entering the world with nothing and leaving with nothing became a common Jewish saying that Paul borrows as he reasons with Timothy about the contented life.

"Timothy," he is saying, "remember this. Remember that we were birthed into this world naked, bringing absolutely nothing with us. And we will exit this life taking absolutely nothing with us. Remember this, Timothy, as you reflect on what you think you need. We enter the world with nothing. We leave with nothing." Feel the weight of this pronouncement. Its gravity is intended to sober us as we measure the time and energy spent accumulating stuff.

From time to time I realize that the things I buy wear out and get old. But the sobering reminder here is that *I* will wear out and get old. And when my body totally gives out and my family buries me, none of the dear objects in my garage, my closets, and my basement will travel with me. My wonderful house, my car, my treasured bike, my many books, my backpacking paraphernalia—these are only temporarily in my custody. If they don't wear out and leave me, I will wear out and leave them.

I remember clearly when this reality first struck me. Many years ago, while attending a conference in another state, I rented a car and drove two hours to a retirement home to visit my aged grandmother. Because of her advanced years, her hearing and sight were almost entirely gone. Her homey room contained a bed, a chair, and maybe a TV but little else. With her life restricted by the effects of old age and poor health, all she needed now could be contained in a single, uncluttered room with a couple pieces of furniture.

The visit jolted me. I thought of how parents come home from the hospital and place their precious newborn in a simple nursery with a crib and a rocker. And now here I was, visiting a loved one on the other end of the journey whose material accoutrements amounted to a bed and a rocker in a retirement home room. As I climbed into the car and began the two-hour drive back, I was hit by a question: How much stuff is it really necessary to accumulate between these two rooms? How much do we need to have to feel as if we are enough? To feel full? To say "I'm satisfied now"? In consideration of the realities marking our beginning and end, I judge that the amount of junk we surround ourselves with is insane.

And Paul reasons, "Timothy. Listen to me. We come in with nothing. We leave with nothing. There is little certainty in life, but one certainty is that we brought nothing in and we will take nothing out. Timothy, do not become obsessed with gathering things around yourself that you cannot keep. Remember this when you stroll through the massive shopping district of Ephesus. Recall this as boats unload their goods in the harbor. As you and your people are tempted by an endless variety of products for sale, don't be seduced by the empty promise that another purchase will complete you. It won't and it can't. Find your life in the Giver and not in his gifts."

Do not underestimate the power of this way of thinking. The virtue of contentment is utterly liberating. It frees us from the illusion that a purchase can take away our loneliness, fill our emptiness, or heal our brokenness. Speaking for his team, Paul proclaims, "If we have food and clothing, we will be content with that." Now, there's a challenge. With something to wear and something to eat, I will be content. A coat and a sandwich—I'm filled and satisfied. A pair of shoes and a bowl of soup—utterly contented.

As I reflect on these words, I feel as if I'm listening to a foreign language. Because we live in a consumer culture powered by relentless advertising, Paul's words sound almost strange or even wrong. But there is also something in his reflection that feels incredibly freeing. Liberating. We have become enslaved to our stuff, and the road to freedom will require a new language. The language of the contented, satisfied life.

02

Time to Enroll

7 lbs., 6 oz.

Josh and Sara had a plan. That was before their lives were radically reshaped by 7 lbs., 6 oz. They never imagined how this tiny baby daughter would alter their lives. Before her arrival, they had decided that Sara would continue to work full-time outside the home. When they discussed their plans, she mused, "I love my work, and I don't see myself leaving my career to be with the baby all day. I just don't think I'm the stay-at-home-mom type." The plan was to take two months off when the baby came, rest up, heal up, get into a new rhythm, and then return to full-time work with a daily child-care routine. Then Maggie arrived and changed everything. As each day passed, Sara increasingly came to dread leaving her baby girl all day, every day, and returning to fulltime work outside the home.

One decisive evening she firmly announced, "I'm not going back to work full-time." A bit stunned, Josh argued, "But this was our plan." Sara countered simply by repeating herself with increased intensity and volume: "I'm *not* going back to work full-time!" It appeared that a decision had been made, from which his wife was unlikely to budge.

Now the real number crunching begins on a long Thursday night at the dining room table equipped with legal pad, pencils, and calculator. If they drop from two full incomes, they will need to embrace corresponding adjustments in lifestyle. The evening at the table is only the first round of budget cuts.

What will they release, relinquish, give up? Perhaps their annual, two-week summer vacation at the cottage. Maybe the frequency with which they dine out, which with their current work schedule is perpetual. They had dreamed of moving out of their "starter home" after a couple of years. Now those plans will have to be delayed—or shelved indefinitely. And they will actually be pressed into a budget for clothing, gifts, and household items.

They never imagined 7 lbs., 6 oz. would change their lives like this. Josh and Sara have just enrolled in the school of contentment.

As they move into a new season, how will God's grace prevail, empowering them to live deeply satisfied lives as they release luxuries and amend their purchasing habits? Can the living Christ grant joy and peace as they cut back and cut down, as they embrace new dreams?

Don't underestimate their challenge. Their task is not merely to live more simply but to simplify their lives with a bearing of grace and joy. Don't confuse simplicity with contentment. On one hand, one can simplify out of necessity but do so with a cankerous attitude. Contentment, on the other hand, is not simply living with less. Remember, contentment is a satisfied heart, a spirit that is alive to God and to others, whether or not we have what we desire. Contentment is being fully alive whatever our situation. What a miracle it is when contentment rescues us from resentment in a season of cutting back.

The Gift of Contentment

- A divorce sends a suddenly single mother of two spinning into a time of shortage.
- A stretch of prolonged unemployment for a family demands a radically curtailed lifestyle.
- Fed up with mounting debt, a couple drastically cut expenses in an attempt to free themselves from financial slavery.

For each person—each situation—there is the opportunity to enroll in the school of contentment. The stakes are high. Particularly during a season of shortage, the most natural response is resentment over our situation. Discomfort can easily boil over into self- pity. "Why is this happening to me?" "Why do we struggle when others have it so easy?" A spirit of complaint can sweep over us, polluting our spirit and poisoning our attitude.

Some circumstances prove so difficult that it is impossible for the heart to remain neutral. Contentment combats the downward drift of the heart. It is through contentment that we encounter fullness in a period of shortage, and joy in a journey of downscaling.

Often we are unwillingly thrown into a season of cutting back, as in the case of sudden job loss. But this same spirit of contentment, of being satisfied, comes into play when we amend our lifestyle by choice. Life-giving contentment guides us as we abandon trivial spending to make a wise, strategic purchase or when we determine that it is time to hunker down and build savings instead of frittering away our paycheck week after week. God-given contentment is also a precious gift when we place a moratorium on significant purchases so that we can fully embrace a time of increased giving.

Enrolling

Over the years, Chris and I have willingly enrolled in the school of contentment a number of times. On three of these occasions we entered a "spending fast"—once to make a strategic purchase, once to build strategic savings, and once to give a strategic gift. Each occasion meant being content with what we owned for a lengthy period of time. I share these stories in the hope that they will encourage and motivate you. If you find yourself in a period of opportunity when you simply have to make do, know that you are not alone.

The Down Payment

We fell in love with the small brick house, its mature oaks towering above the yard. Chris and I were both twenty-two, a year into marriage, serving a tiny church, and broke. Yet we somehow thought that home ownership might be within our grasp. The sellers, enduring a difficult housing market and increasingly weary because of a property that refused to sell, agreed to let us move in and rent for twelve months with the stipulation that we come up with the down payment within a year. As I recall, our combined income that year was in the neighborhood of $18,000. To fulfill our obligation, we needed to squirrel away $7,000 for the down payment and live on the remainder, which meant that we could buy *nothing*. We signed a contract and enrolled in the school of contentment.

All discretionary income, every available dollar, went to a single goal: the down payment for our first home. During this twelve-month period, we forsook restaurants—even fast food—we took no vacation, and we have no memory of purchasing new clothing. I distinctly remember standing in the beverage aisle of a local grocery store reasoning with a 2-liter bottle of Coca-Cola that was on sale. "I know you're only 89 cents, but I can't buy you. The almost dollar I would spend on you should go toward the house. I'll be back in a year, and perhaps I can enjoy your company then." We learned to be content with very little as we stretched toward a worthy financial goal.

In relating the story of that thrifty year, I do not wish to leave you with the impression that this level of discipline has typified our financial lives. I doubt there has been another phase when we exercised such care in monitoring the destination of every single dollar. It is a bit embarrassing to confess, but I fear that the apex of my financial discipline may have been as a twenty-two-year-old. But the reward for enrolling in the school of contentment? Sitting across from the sellers at the title company a year later and closing on our first home.

Emergency Fund

It is certain that we will need to enroll in contentment school more than once. Graduating with honors in one season of life is no guarantee of receiving passing grades in another. Years passed after we moved into our first home, and our family grew to include our three children, Sarah, Andrew, and Alex. We worked hard to spend wisely, limit debt, and give faithfully. During this time, Chris and I began meeting with a group of friends to complete a biblically based financial study.

It was the perfect time for this endeavor as we were making the final payments on a minivan and rapidly paying off modest credit card debt. Other than our mortgage, we were about to become totally debt free. Nearing this finish line, we drafted a mental list of long-delayed purchases—things we desired to buy once we reached this long-anticipated goal. I forget all that was on our wish list, but I remember that it included new living room furniture to replace the well-worn, mismatched assortment of pieces that had accumulated over time.

Then one night the topic of our study exposed a gaping hole in our financial profile: *savings*, and specifically the need for an emergency fund. Financial counselors advise an emergency fund for those unexpected and uninvited episodes. The furnace goes out, the car transmission malfunctions, a medical expense sends us reeling, the refrigerator refuses to fridge—and suddenly, with no margin, we find ourselves back in debt as we scramble to cover the emergency. Wisdom calls for setting funds aside for such eventualities. Many prudent advisors suggest that an emergency fund also cover at least three months of routine living expenses in case of a loss of income. Chris and I had saved nothing. Nada. We were about to become debt free but had no money in reserve.

Again we enrolled in the school of contentment, seeking to be satisfied with what we had until we saved an emergency fund. We delayed all significant purchases for over a year—

our collage of beat-up furniture would simply have to serve another year of duty. We had a goal that was more strategic than having nice furniture, and we learned to be content with what we had until this goal was reached.

Saving requires delaying a purchase today so that we have resources tomorrow. Many of us never save because we are simply unwilling to live contentedly with what we have so that money can be redirected for future needs.

The Building and the Buick

A third time we enrolled in the school of contentment (though not the last) was so we could give a strategic gift. Our church was in the throes of a major building program. The purchase of over sixty acres and the dream of a new campus demanded intense focus and sacrifice. Chris and I made a three-year financial commitment that really stretched us. We simply couldn't give the gift we desired to give while buying things we intended to buy. So to give sacrificially, we privately vowed that we would not purchase a better automobile until our three-year building fund commitment was fulfilled. This did not feel like a sacrifice at the time because our car was in great shape. But our faithful Buick decided to disintegrate the moment we made this quiet pledge. The sun-beaten dash began to crack, the roof fabric started to sag, and patches of leprous rust steadily ate away at the car's body.

This time, contentment meant patiently enduring a rapidly eroding vehicle as we systematically gave the offering we had covenanted to give.

I know in the grand scheme of things this probably sounds trivial, but driving that aging Buick month after month was an important part of our journey. Remember that we were not short on cash; we were just giving the money away. I think this is an important story to tell, because so often Christians are tempted to give in a way that costs them nothing. Our propensity is to buy what we want to buy and then give out of what is left over. Chris and I were aware, however, that this gift was costing us something—every time we climbed into the Buick and pulled out of the driveway.

Looking back, this is one of the best investments we ever made. Cars come and go, inevitably occupying their assigned place in a junk pile. But the facility our church constructed has become home to thousands of people whose lives have been enriched and deepened in a lasting way. Enduring the minor inconvenience of an older vehicle for a few years was nothing when compared with the profound movement of God that has occurred in our new church home.

The Ongoing Struggle

Graduation from the school of contentment is not final. In one season of life, we enroll, struggle, and grow—only to enroll again in another season. Learning contentment is a lifetime journey.

I'm certain that many of you reading this chapter are embarking on a time of cutting back financially, perhaps because of a recent financial earthquake. It is also possible that many of you plan to alter spending habits to become more disciplined in saving or giving. Whatever your motivation for embracing new habits and patterns, I pray that you will discover the freedom of contentment and come to know the liberation of the satisfied life.

03

Trapped, Drowning, and Bleeding

The Promotion

Jake sits in the dim family room long after Laura and the girls have gone to bed. The promotion was offered on Friday and he was given the weekend to "think things over." It's late Sunday night and he's still thinking. The two sides of an imaginary set of scales move up and down as he weighs both the obvious and potential benefits against the probable costs.

On one side of the scales he places the 28 percent raise, the house this raise would afford, and the title that accompanies this new position. On the other side of the scales he places the inevitable upheaval of another move to a new city.

Jake chose a sales position with this growing company because of the promise of "rapid promotion for motivated people." Jake is motivated and promotions have come fairly rapidly. Laura is a successful webpage designer, and she can work anywhere she has Internet access. But for Jake, seizing this opportunity will require relocation.

Three years earlier this would have been a simple decision, but now Jake is literally losing sleep over the matter. What intensifies his dilemma is how healthy the family has become in their current setting. With two stable incomes, they already earn more than enough to meet their needs. The girls are doing great in school. Laura has established some deep friendships. And the family is finally anchored in a church they love and enjoying a spiritual depth they've never experienced before. They are thriving here financially, emotionally, and spiritually. For the first time in their married lives, Jake and Laura feel rooted.

But a 28 percent raise! And with the possibility of additional promotion should he succeed in his new post. But if he uproots the family and succeeds, will that simply lead to additional uprooting and moving and succeeding? Is there a finish line out there somewhere?

If someone had asked him directly, "Jake, your family is doing phenomenally well here. Are you willing to compromise their health for more money?" he would have immediately answered "no." But clearly, his honest answer is, "I don't know. That's why I'm still awake, trying to decide."

Never Enough

In response to Jake's question, "Is there a finish line out there somewhere?" the answer is a resounding "no." Not if our quest is for "more." If our goal is more, then whatever we have is never enough. It is like running a race where a finish line doesn't exist.

A millennium before the time of Paul, wealthy King Solomon of Jerusalem penned this convicting proverb on the limited satisfaction of increased income.

> Whoever loves money never has enough;
> whoever loves wealth is never satisfied with their income.
>
> (Ecclesiastes 5:10)

Was this Solomon's personal testimonial? Did he learn this truth through experience? Reflect on your own life and journey. Have you ever had a pay raise that delivered unending satisfaction? Of course not. Can you testify that a new income level—or house, or car, or whatever—provided immediate short-term satisfaction but that the newness wore off in time? I'm certain you can. Is there not a propensity to lose that full, "I have enough now" sensation? Solomon's proverb echoes down to our generation: "Whoever loves wealth is never satisfied with their income." Ouch! So true.

Chasing the Wind

Solomon described accumulation as "wind chasing." He undertook countless expansive projects, built many elaborate houses, and planted miles of vineyards. He cultivated gardens and parks and orchards. He owned more herds and flocks than anyone in Jerusalem before him and amassed piles of silver and gold. Though he seems to have enjoyed aspects of his work, when he surveyed the accumulated sum of all he had accomplished, he called it "a chasing after the wind" (Ecclesiastes 2:11).

Wind chasing is a masterful image. I picture running around my backyard, grabbing at the rushing air. "Got it," I exclaim as I close my fist. I slowly open my hand, uncurling one finger at a time and … there's nothing there. "I had it! What happened?" This is the mental image the wealthy king chose to describe his massive building programs and chests of gold. His quest for fulfillment through accumulation led to this self-indictment: "Wind Chaser."

With each promotion, raise, and move, could Jake be chasing the wind? Is it possible that he is trying to catch something that isn't catchable?

The temptation to compromise spiritual movement to chase money is not unique to Jake. The thirst for wealth is a common cause of spiritual wreckage.

Assessing the Damage

Those who want to get rich fall into temptation and a trap and into many foolish and harmful desires that plunge

people into ruin and destruction. For the love of money
is a root of all kinds of evil. Some people, eager for money,
have wandered from the faith and pierced themselves
with many griefs. (1 Timothy 6:9–10)

With these ominous words, Paul's challenge about the contented, satisfied life takes a tone of urgency. He reminds Timothy of the destruction and heartache that have come from the headlong, obsessive, quest for more. Trapped, drowning, and bleeding—these were some of the descriptors Paul used to portray the self-inflicted predicaments and wounds of people entangled in the never-ending pursuit of more wealth. Paul compiles a series of graphic images to describe our peril when we cannot break free from unbridled longing to increase our financial status.

He speaks of falling into a trap, plunging into ruin, and being pierced with grief. Trapped, drowning, and bleeding. This is vivid, graphic language. It is clear that Paul wants Timothy to recognize the spiritual devastation that occurs when we fail to harness the power of contentment. The quest to fill the empty space with stuff is not simply illusive but can be self-destroying.

Observe Paul's words carefully. He does not counsel Timothy that "money is the root of evil" but rather that *the love of money* is a root of all kinds of evil. What he warns about here are the cravings of those who "want to get rich" and "are eager for money." He describes an intense craving for wealth that can result in spiritual bankruptcy. Is it just me, or does anyone else find these words deeply convicting and challenging? As I reflect on this warning I wonder, "How can I earn money, save money, spend money, and invest money... but not fall in love with money?" If we deal with this question honestly, I think we must confess that this is a huge challenge in our culture and is likely to be a lifelong battle for all of us.

We don't have to look far to bear personal witness to the self-inflicted wounds and peril Paul forecasted. We cram our lives with stuff, compound the clutter, and believe that a little more, just a little more, will finally fill the empty space. We attempt to fill an emotional-spiritual vacuum with a variety of objects, and then we become disillusioned when our efforts fail to produce the lasting fullness we chased. Instead of changing tactics, we simply swap things—if a new house doesn't do it, perhaps an extravagant vacation will. And if a resort fails to do the trick, perhaps a pricey cottage will. I am not making a case here against home or cottage ownership, and vacations can provide much-needed rest and re-create the soul. What we should be concerned about is what we believe these things will do for us. We ask them to fill a void they cannot possibly fill. Disappointed, we move on to the next thing. We race faster, work harder, earn more, spend more, perhaps save more, and like Jake, wonder if there is a finish line.

Speaking about this headlong quest for more, Paul offered the sorrowful observation, "Some people, eager for money, have wandered from the faith" (v. 10). Remember that Ephesus was the economic hub of the region—a center for buying and selling. And there were some in the Jesus community in Ephesus who, in their money-focused obsession, had wandered far from Christ.

Paul uses strong language to seize Timothy's attention. "Timothy," he seems to be saying, "pay attention, lift your chin, look at the carnage. Some have wandered, strayed, drifted from Christ because of this. There are those who are no longer walking with Jesus because something else got their attention. Don't let this happen to you. Don't let this happen to your people. Many will sacrifice their spiritual lives on the altar of accumulation."

The mention of individuals whose financial dreams derailed their spiritual progress should not surprise us. It is impossible to be a fully devoted follower of Jesus and simultaneously be a fully devoted seeker of accumulation. Jesus assured, "No one can serve two masters ... You cannot serve both God and money" (Matthew 6:24). One will inevitably win out over the other. Each competes to master our energy, dreams, allegiance, and devotion.

As you read this, if you feel you are trapped, drowning, or bleeding, I want so much for you to experience the joy of contentment and the grace of generosity instead. I want for you to be freed from this treadmill. I so deeply want you to enjoy what you have without being deceived into thinking that it can fill something it was never designed to fill or fix something it was never intended to fix.

04

Not Alone

The Long Drive Home

Kyle travels northeast from Phoenix to Minneapolis. Though this is a twenty-five-hour journey, he drives the distance straight through, pausing only for fuel and occasional fast food. As the miles click by, he repeats the depressive sentence, "I can't believe I'm moving back in with my parents." This single line has wormed through his mind since packing the last of his belongings and dropping off the keys to his apartment. After being on his own for seven years, he still can't quite believe that he's moving back to his old neighborhood, to his parents' house, and—groan—to his old bedroom.

Shortly after turning eighteen, Kyle headed off to college. Apart from Christmas breaks and a few summer vacations, he has been mostly on his own ever since. Following graduation, he landed a position with a design firm in Phoenix that specialized in custom homes. He rented a two-bedroom apartment with a friend from college and began his new, independent life in Arizona.

With the plunge of the Phoenix housing market, new home construction slowed to a crawl and with it the high demand for new home design. Kyle was bumped from full-time to "as needed" status. The hours became highly inconsistent, sometimes a forty-hour week but then followed by a twelve-hour week. His cash flow worsened when his roommate moved out of state, leaving him fully responsible for the monthly rent. Finally, two consecutive weeks passed with no work at all as business moved from sluggish to stalled. There are doubts that his firm will recover anytime in the near future.

Throughout the turn of events, Kyle was honest with his parents about how things were actually going. In weekly Sunday afternoon phone conversations, he shared both the initial excitement over his new opportunities and then his discouragement as these opportunities began to dry up. As the situation worsened, they began hinting about him returning home for a spell and perhaps rebooting his career in Minneapolis. "We've got a big, quiet house that we rattle around in, and we would love to spend some time with you." At first Kyle vehemently declined, but as vocational options evaporated in the Arizona heat, their offer began to make sense. After repeated refusal, logic kicked in. He has far more connections in Minneapolis and, quite frankly, it feels like home.

And so he travels northeast through the night and repeats the phrase that drapes over him like ill-fitting clothes: "Well …

for now … I'm living with my parents while job hunting." He imagines reciting this confession as he bumps into old family friends who ask what he's up to. Sweet and sour. His parents' kind generosity seasoned with the tang of humiliation.

As he drives through the darkness of Kansas, Kyle also experiences a wave of gratitude. "My parents are good people. I'm thankful to have a place to land. Is this God's way of providing for me?" Though frustrated by the turn of events, he feels deeply blessed. This sense of gratefulness is the front edge of the journey of contentment—a yearlong journey he will navigate as he re-anchors at home, reengages with old friends, and seeks guidance and provision in a job search.

What will Kyle make of this time? And what will this time make of Kyle? From some sermon in his past, he remembers the words, "Peace cannot be stolen without your consent. You willingly yield it up." He resolves that this difficult phase of his life will not rob him of joy and gratitude.

The car rolls into Iowa, edging toward home. He shoots a prayer upward. "God, please help me be thankful. Please help me bless my parents as long as I am with them. Please guide my job hunting. Please get me out of this fast because this is not where I want to be!"

Kyle has just enrolled in the school of contentment. So far, he is receiving passing grades. The voice of contentment whispers, "It's possible to live a life of deep joy while not having everything you want." The school of contentment leads the heart to find deep peace and thanksgiving, fullness, and rest, even when traveling through an unwanted detour. But note that Kyle's dilemma is not exclusively financial. Money issues are certainly in play, but the emotional challenge also encompasses his relocation, his job search, and possible embarrassment when confessing that he has moved back with his parents.

Life-giving contentment can sustain you through a severe financial setback, but it is also a crucial ally if you are recovering from a surgery or experiencing what seems like an interminable delay. One of the greatest challenges to contentment is when we are waiting for a situation to change.

Humidity

One month down. Eleven months to go.

Heather made a commitment to serve for a year at a Spanish-speaking school in Honduras. The decision was made because of the compelling pictures on the school's website. But though photographs may adequately portray children and buildings, they are a poor medium for conveying the smells, the reality of this new world—and the oppressive humidity. When Heather stepped off the plane, the hot, damp air hit her like a board in the face. Her home, Palm Springs, California, has been described as having "a dry heat." Suddenly she comprehends this expression for the first time as she experiences the opposite: everything is damp all the time. She feels perpetually wet and wonders if this is something one can grow accustomed to or whether it must simply be endured as the months unfold.

The climate is not Heather's only source of discomfort. A wave of homesickness crashes over her as she begins her second month of teaching, not simply missing her family but longing for those familiar things that home represents—food, friends, and conversation in her own language. As she settles into a daily routine, Heather realizes this is not going to be the adventure she imagined. But she determines to honor her full-year commitment.

In an encouraging email, a friend attempts to lift her spirits. He draws her attention to Philippians 4:11–12, citing Paul's powerful words: "I have learned to be content whatever the circumstances ... in any and every situation ..." What Heather finds riveting is the reminder that these words on finding contentment were penned by someone in prison. Heather muses on the words again. "Contentment ... whatever the circumstances ... in any and every situation." That would include the wet heat and missing home while in Honduras.

Heather grabs her Bible and reads the surrounding verses.

I have learned to be content whatever the circumstances. I know what it is to be in need, and I know what it is to have plenty. I have learned the secret of being content in any and every situation, whether well fed or hungry, whether living in plenty or in want. I can do all this through him who gives me strength. (Philippians 4:11–13)

She chews on these words, mulling them over phrase by phrase. "Whether well fed or hungry, whether living in plenty or in want." The imprisoned apostle claimed that he learned to be content in times of extreme discomfort—gnawed by hunger, living with woefully inadequate provision. When he wrote to the Philippians, Paul had completed three lengthy church planting journeys, traveling thousands of miles on foot and by sea. He had experienced frequent arrests, severe floggings, shipwrecks, dangerous river crossings, muggings, hunger, thirst, and cold, sleepless nights (see 2 Corinthians 11:24–27). Heather reflects on the fact that Paul spoke these powerful words on contentment from deeply personal experience.

As she scans the verses again, a three-word confession jumps out at her: "I have learned." It appears twice in this brief section. Paul states that he *learned* the secret of being content." Apparently, contentment is not something you are born with. It is not like entering the world with blue eyes or red hair. Heather suspects that learning contentment will be as challenging as mastering a foreign language. Her life at home was so comfortable. Will gaining fluency in contentment feel like her first fumbling attempts at learning Spanish?

How did the apostle graciously endure nagging hunger or

miserable sleepless nights? How did he survive repeated flogging without becoming mean, nasty, and caustic? Where did
such strength come from? Paul's answer explains: "I didn't
have the strength. I could only achieve contentment with the
strength of Christ. I needed Jesus very, very badly."

Heather reads and re-reads the final line: "I can do all this
through him who gives me strength." Heather has known this
verse for years—it is often quoted in a variety of settings—
but she never realized that it was written in the context of
Paul's learning contentment in seasons of hardship. Here
Paul credits his contented life with the strength given by the
resurrected Christ. Within himself alone the apostle did not
have the resources to live the satisfied, joyful life, particularly
during times of extreme discomfort. He needed outside help.
The strength of Christ empowered him. Heather finds herself
tearing up a bit as she realizes, "I am not alone."

The brief email from her friend and the reflection it
spawns are truly life-giving. Heather concedes that her challenge is not simply to grit her teeth and endure the year but to
embrace a life of joy and thankfulness in an environment she
finds uncomfortable, alien, and lonely. While musing over the
email she contemplates a life-giving question, of a life-giving
God: "What could it look like to live a deeply satisfied life in
a profoundly uncomfortable setting?" Heather has enrolled in
the school of contentment.

One month down. Eleven to go.

He's with You

Reflect again on Paul's words: "I can do all this through him who gives me strength." You are not alone. You may draw upon the strength of Christ to pull off what you could never do on your own. The strength of Christ is available ...

If you adjust from two incomes to one.

As you turn the sharp corner from "buy now, pay later" to careful savings and deferred gratification.

When you turn from obsessive saving to systematic generosity.

If a foreclosure moves you from dream house to small apartment.

As you stare into a cluttered garage and crammed closet, knowing you buy things you don't need and don't use but feeling incapable of curbing your spending.

His strength is available to you as you enroll in the school of contentment. You are not alone.

PART 1: The School of Contentment

Reflect and Discuss:

1. What's the danger of living without contentment spiritually? Materially? Relationally?

2. Was there a season in your life when you when learned to be content with a situation?

Project: Count your shirts and shoes

Include sweaters, athletic, casual, and T-shirts. Include athletic shoes, sandals, and flip-flops. This exercise is not intended to inspire guilt but simply to aid you in seeing the stuff that piles up around you. Do you detect any patterns in your world of accumulation?

Consider this experience and write about it or share your reflections with your small group.

Project: Give something away

You have something in your life that is of value to someone yet goes unused by you. To whom could this item be given? The breadmaker or set of crystal that collects dust in your kitchen. The bike rack or tent that does nothing but occupy space in your garage or basement. Who might be delighted to possess something that goes unused in your household? Find its rightful owner. Give it away this week.

Comparison

05

Conflict in the Vineyard

Starter Home

Matt and Alicia survey the shaded backyard to determine the ideal location for a swing set. Their first child is due in three months, and they share immense gratification over buying their first house. After living in a cramped apartment for four years, they finally amassed enough cash for a down payment and discovered a bargain on this two-bedroom home nestled in a quaint neighborhood. Alicia becomes giddy whenever she utters the words "our house."

Closing on the property and moving in was just the beginning. Though the structure is sound, the home is dowdy. Definitely dated. Tired. The kitchen pleads for updating, the landscaping suffers from neglect, and the carpet has seen better days. Matt has three months to transform a dark, wood-paneled den into a cheery baby's bedroom. But these other cosmetic improvements can be made over time as money becomes available.

It's Friday evening. They walk the dozen feet to their

detached garage, which houses their aging but reliable car. The absence of any recent automotive repair increases their sense of gratitude. As they pull away from their treasured home, they share deep thankfulness for what God has provided — a strong sensation that God, in his goodness, has blessed them immensely. They feel full. They feel rich.

Their destination is a short, fifteen-minute drive to the home of friends they haven't seen since college graduation. They obediently follow the turns directed by their GPS. The staccato female voice guides them to a cul-de-sac with newer houses and the manicured front yard of their friends' house. The door to the attached garage is open, displaying two newer vehicles. Initial hugs and greetings at the front door segue into a quick tour. The entryway reveals an open floor plan, the smartly decorated living area flowing seamlessly into the kitchen, which hosts stainless steel appliances amid granite countertops. Alicia admires, "What a beautiful kitchen." Matt wonders, "How in the world are they affording this?" Upstairs are the bedrooms with a master suite and walk-in closets.

It's a beautiful evening, and they enjoy an unrushed dinner together on the cobblestone patio in the backyard. The patio furniture does not appear to have been purchased at a garage sale.

Three hours later, Matt and Alicia climb into their faithful car and return home. The ride is a bit subdued. They pull into their driveway feeling ... well, feeling poor. Gone is the sense of fullness they experienced just a few hours before. In fact, there is an inner suspicion that God has ripped them off.

Okay, what just happened? How can the heart shift from deep gratitude to subtle resentment in three short hours? The answer—in a word—is *comparison*. Comparison rarely enjoys what one has but instead dwells on what someone else has and, consequently, obsesses over what one lacks. If you succumb to comparison like this, prepare to wave good-bye to those higher, treasured attributes we seek to cultivate. Comparison is a thief and a killer. Comparison robs you of gratitude and contentment. Comparison massacres joy. Another casualty of comparison is generosity. We are drawn to give generously when we experience a sense of abundance, when we become aware of the blessings that surround us. As Matt and Alicia drive back to their new home, feeling poor, any impulse to live generously has just taken a huge hit. Comparison is the enemy of the satisfied, generous life.

Conflict in the Vineyard

In Matthew, chapter 20, Jesus spoke of the sinister nature of comparison in a parable he told when heading toward Jerusalem near the end of his life and ministry. When his loyal disciples inquired about what reward they might expect for abandoning their homes and jobs to follow him, Jesus assured them they would, indeed, be rewarded. But then he added an unexpected story that strikes at the heart of the lethal effects of living by comparison.

> For the kingdom of heaven is like a landowner who went out early in the morning to hire workers for his vineyard. He agreed to pay them a denarius for the day and sent them into his vineyard.　　　　　(Matthew 20:1–2)

A town sputters to life at dawn. The owner of a vineyard heads to the marketplace in the town square to hire day laborers to assist in harvesting his crop. When grapes ripen, harvesting them on time becomes a matter of urgency. In this first century, the marketplace serves as the town's "temp agency." The landowner encounters men seeking work and negotiates a fair wage. He offers to pay a denarius for a full day's work, and the men agree to that arrangement. A denarius is a small silver coin that is the standard day's pay for a soldier or unskilled laborer.

Off to the vineyard they go. The sun is barely up when their work begins. The hours between six and nine in the morning are cool as the sun has yet to reach its full intensity. Dew from the night before reduces the dust. Perhaps the men have slept well and are refreshed as they begin their day. These early hours pass rapidly.

Then the story turns. At nine o'clock, the owner leaves his vineyard and heads back to town. Again he scours the marketplace to secure additional workers. But now the financial offer changes. Because a quarter of the workday has elapsed, the owner simply tells the latecomers, "You also go work in my vineyard, and I will pay you whatever is right" (v. 4). This new crop of workers joins those who have already been laboring for three hours.

The temperature rises steadily as noon approaches. While the midday sun beats upon the harvesters, the plot thickens as the owner disappears from his vineyard once again to return to town and augment his workforce. He repeats this scenario of adding workers at three o'clock and finally at five o'clock. The last laborers hired will only toil a single hour before the workday expires.

Walk among the vines as evening approaches. As the day draws to a close, the harvesters are wrapping up their work. Jesus' simple agricultural tale takes an unexpected twist. The vineyard scene is about to turn ugly.

The owner instructs his foreman to pay the workers, beginning with those who arrived last and concluding with those hired first. Imagine the line with me. In front are those who worked a single hour. They hardly broke a sweat. Behind them are those who worked three, six, and nine hours. Finally, in the very back of the line are the truly exhausted. These men, hired at dawn, have endured twelve hours of strenuous labor in the baking sun.

The troubling incident occurs as the men are compensated. We read that "the workers who were hired about five in the afternoon came and each received *a denarius*" (Matthew 20:9, emphasis added). Did you see that? Remember that this small silver coin was the common pay for a day's work. The men who were recruited at the end of the day, who worked a single hour, received a full day's pay, twelve times the amount they expected. There is great excitement in the front of the line, but there is also elation in the back of the line. See the delighted faces of those who were up at the crack of dawn and worked the full twelve hours? If those laboring a single hour received a full day's pay, they are thinking, what reward will be given to those who toiled in the blazing sun since early morning? Those in the back of the line anticipate a huge bonus.

But when those who had served all day are paid, they too receive only a denarius. Those who labored a single hour and those who endured the entire day all receive the same amount. We can see the rage of the weary, sun-beaten workers who put in a full day. They are *livid*—furious that they have been treated equally with those who were hired for a mere hour. Press your ear to the story and listen to them protest. "These who were hired last worked only one hour ... and you have made them equal to us who have borne the burden of the work and the heat of the day" (vv. 11–12). Their collective bellow? "This isn't *fair*!"

But now the owner engages one of his ranting workers. "I am not being unfair to you, friend. Didn't you agree to work for a denarius?" (v. 13). He is saying to them, "Fair? Wait a minute. Did I rip you off? Rewind the tape. Twelve hours ago we stood in the marketplace. I offered to pay you a denarius and you agreed. Here it is. Did I break our agreement? Did I break our contract? Did I scam you? I gave you exactly what we agreed upon."

The vineyard owner continues in verses 14–15: "Take your pay and go. I want to give the one who was hired last the same as I gave you. Don't I have the right to do what I want with my own money?" Tune in to his logic. "It's my money! If I want to throw it away, I can throw it away. If I want to give money to people who didn't show up at all, that's my business. What do you care?" He then cuts to the heart of the matter: "Or are you *envious* because I am generous?" (v. 15, emphasis added).

As I reflect on Jesus' story, I realize that the wounded rage wasn't generated because the twelve-hour workers received too little. The rancor erupted because they thought the one-hour workers were given too much. We are prone to lose our balance, not because we have received less than we deserve but because someone near us has received more than we think *they* deserve. The wounded voice of comparison demands, "Why them and not me?"

06

Ice Cream Bowls

The Problem with More

Let's explore the disruptive nature of comparison through viewing a simple family interaction. On a warm summer evening, Jon calls to his son in the backyard. "How would you like some ice cream?" His son scampers into the house as the half-gallon carton is lifted from the freezer. Moose Tracks, that heavenly blend of vanilla ice cream, swirls of dark fudge, and miniature peanut butter cups—the boy's favorite. A generous scoop is placed in his bowl. All is well with the world.

Now change the scenario slightly. Jon calls two sons in from the backyard and removes two bowls from the cupboard. Jon spoons out a generous scoop for his older son, but in the younger boy's bowl he places *two* scoops. What happens? Suddenly, the harmony of the universe is disrupted. A cosmic injustice has been committed. Comparing the two bowls, the older son wails, "That's not fair!"

Don't overlook the profound teaching imbedded in this simplistic tale of the ice cream bowls. Understand that the issue had nothing to do with what was in the older son's bowl. It's what his brother had in his ice cream bowl that started a war. The problem wasn't that the older brother was given too little but that his younger brother was given more.

Isn't it overly optimistic to assume that this syndrome magically dissipates when we exit childhood? The tendency to live by comparison is alive and well. While deep satisfaction is possible when I focus on my own bowl, complaint erupts when my focus drifts to the "more" in somebody else's bowl. Welcome to the world of soul-destroying comparison. When comparison reigns, the satisfied life evaporates.

House Envy

Let's revisit Matt and Alicia, the couple we met earlier who moved from their cramped apartment into their first home. They pulled out of their driveway experiencing deep gratitude, thankfulness, and a sense that God had blessed them immensely. Hours later, they returned home from an evening at their friends' house, sensing that God is unfair—feeling somehow that they had been ripped off. What happened over the course of this brief evening outing that could possibly cause such an enormous shift in perspective?

Using the ice cream bowl analogy, I suggest that when their focus was on *their* bowl, they saw it heaped with God's goodness, piled high with blessings. It was when they took their eyes off their bowl and fixated on someone else's bowl that their spirit of gratitude was displaced by a demon of complaint. This is the nature of comparison. An obsessive focus on someone else's bowl inevitably kills off gratitude over what is in our bowl. Comparison kills.

Overtime

Consider how swiftly the tide of gratitude shifts when waves of comparison roll in. Lindsey shares a house with two room-mates and experiences financial anxiety common to those in the entry-level job market—they have too many expenses against too few hours of work. And with the approaching Christmas and New Year holidays, her bills and worries compound. In a moment of anxious trust, Lindsey fires off a prayer. "God, I could really use your help here." A well-known fragment from our Lord's Prayer lodges in her mind: "Give us today our daily bread." With this brief, whispered plea, she invites the capable God into her plight.

Lindsey is stunned by the immediacy of God's answer. Days after uttering the petition, her manager pulls her aside in the break room during lunch. Over Christmas and New Year's, so many of their coworkers will be vacationing that the company is in desperate need for other employees to step in and fill the gaps. Would Lindsey have any interest in work-ing overtime during the holiday season? She expresses her eagerness and gratitude. In addition to her usual hours, she will work Christmas Eve, New Year's Eve, and New Year's Day. With this single conversation Lindsey feels a shift in her financial center of gravity. She will cancel social engagements with friends and work through the holidays. A weight lifts from her life.

As she drives away from work she prays, "Thank you." The experience in her car can only be described as pure, unadulterated worship. "God, *thank you.* I prayed, and you *provided*—thank you so *very much* for paying attention. You truly see, you listen, you provide." She can't wait to share the news with her two roommates. When she springs up the porch steps and enters the living room, she finds that an animated conversation is underway. One roommate gushes, "My parents are vacationing in Paris over New Year's and asked me to join them. I'm so excited! I've never been to Paris in the winter."

Her second roommate interjects, "You are so lucky. We go to the same resort in Colorado year, after year, after year."

Lindsey remains wordless, but is silently seething as she thinks, "I hate both of you." She works while others play. She scrapes by while others enjoy luxuries so far from her own experience. She sulks in her room, bearing a strong suspicion that God is not fair—the universal deck is stacked against her. She feels deprived and overlooked.

What just happened? Over the course of a twenty-minute

drive, her focus was on her own bowl—containing answered prayer, opportunity to work, and financial provision. As she focused on the bowls of her roommates, comparison waged its ugly war and joy was crushed. Thankfulness killed.

Comparison is a destroyer of gratitude and contentment. But its tentacles can reach far beyond disenchantment over houses and vacations. Consider its potential to derail growing faith.

The Company Picnic

On a warm summer Saturday, they drive to the company picnic. Jill reaches over and pats Ben's hand tenderly. She is so pleased with this season of their marriage and with Ben's spiritual progress. Though Ben is no spiritual giant, there is positive movement and solid direction. And he's spending more time with their three children, clearly tuning in more at home. As their van navigates toward the park, she smiles at him. He's growing. She's thankful.

As the afternoon unfolds at the corporate outing, Jill mingles. Extremely extroverted, she chats easily with new acquaintances. She meets, she greets, she chats. She compares. Jill casually interacts with men more ambitious than Ben, who keep themselves in better shape, are perhaps better read, are a bit better dressed, and probably better paid.

She observes their wives. Most of them aren't more attractive than she is, and certainly not as congenial. Uninvited and unedited, a thought steals into her mind. "I could have caught a guy like that …"

Are you stunned by how far the heart traveled in such a brief period of time? Jill's sense of deep gratitude drifted toward this dark impulse when she took her eyes off her own bowl. In this picnic parable, the sinister culprit was comparison. Understand something: the heart that believes God has ripped it off can justify *anything*. If you believe in the core of your being that God is not good, that he is holding out on you or that he is scamming you, you can rationalize *any* behavior.

Comparison is a destroyer. It can easily kill off growing faith. Trust is the glue that holds any relationship together, and if you fundamentally distrust God's goodness, it is highly unlikely that you will follow his leadership in your life. After all, why would you follow someone who is unfair to you?

The First Temptation

Let's begin at the beginning. In the early pages of the Bible we are introduced to the story of Adam and Eve and, with them, the first temptation. Flourishing in an abundant garden, they may dine on the fruit of every tree but one. They enjoy crisp apples or taste tangy oranges. The amazing variety of pomegranates, apricots, and figs is available for their pleasure.

In a world of such delight, how could the tempter possibly

turn their hearts against their creator? Simple. By shifting their focus from what they have to what they lack. "My dear Eve, have you considered the singular object the creative one is withholding from you? Do not gaze upon what he has given. Fix your eyes instead upon what he has withheld. Now, desire ... deeply desire that. God isn't really good. He is holding out on you. Do not focus on what you have but instead upon what you lack."

And Adam and Eve, our first parents, fell. And we, their children, stumble when we compare. Comparison seduces us to obsess over what is withheld while blinding us to the myriad blessings God has given for our enjoyment. Look at the footprints of our trespasses. I think most sin can be traced back to an inner suspicion that God is not good. The more you flirt with comparison, the more tenuous your trusting relationship with God. You simply won't trust him if you suspect he is holding out on you. And you will not follow the God you do not trust, at least not for long. Comparison strangles surging faith. The heart that feels God is not fair begins a slow and steady drift.

07

The Spending Gap

The Neighbors

On a practical financial level, you will discover that comparison wages war with your quest for financial freedom. One of our barriers to thinking sanely about our wealth is that so many people around us don't. And we so often reflexively compare our lifestyles to theirs.

Imagine two families with identical incomes living side by side in a suburban neighborhood. Each family has a combined income of $100,000 a year. (This income may seem incredibly high or extremely inadequate to you. I've picked this figure for easy math purposes. The exact figure is irrelevant to the point I am making.) The family to your left—the Smiths—have devoted themselves to a generations-old financial practice called the 80/10/10 discipline. This spending plan is not their invention but something their grandparents adopted. It is the discipline of restricting their spending to 80 percent of their earnings. They meticulously save 10 percent of their income and 10 percent is generously given away. Sticking to this disciplined plan, the Smiths will spend $80,000 this year.

Now, let's say their neighbors to your right have never practiced such an "absurd" discipline. Instead, the Wilsons are "normal." They too earn a combined income of $100,000 a year but routinely overspend what they are making. They annually spend $105,000, their expenses — clothing, cars, dining out, and vacations — out-distancing their earnings by $5,000 a year.

So, here's the math problem: What is the *earning gap* between the Smiths and the Wilsons? Nothing — the incomes are identical. But what is the *spending gap* between these two families? Annually, the Wilsons are spending $25,000 more than the Smiths, and this purchasing difference will manifest itself in observable ways. This spending gap is real and not theoretical. It is visible. It could show up in the form of golf outings, restaurants, Christmas presents, summer vacations, ski trips, clothing, newer automobiles, recreational vehicles, appliances, landscaping, and home improvements. By saying "yes" to $25,000 of stuff annually that the Smiths are saying "no" to, the Wilsons will simply have more or better stuff or enjoy more frequent or elaborate vacations.

Because of this, when peering over the fence, the Smiths may feel … well, poor. There will be the propensity to look next door and ask, "What's wrong with us? Why can't we go where they go? Why can't we do what they do? Why are our appliances older, and why is our vacation simpler?" The quest for financial sanity will require a powerful statement from the Smiths. They will need to cast a glance next door and clearly concede, "You win. We are not even playing the same game. We will not compete with you and we will not succumb to the temptation to keep up with you. You win."

But this fact remains: for the time being, contentment will feel like a losing proposition. The pursuit of the satisfied life comes at a cost. Around us are real people buying real things. Some of these people are neighbors, work associates, and—I hate to break this news—your sister and brother-in-law. There could be moments when you feel as if you are losing or, more poignantly, you may feel like a loser.

My point is that we may talk about comparison in abstract terms and readily sign off, reasoning that it is a poor idea. But realize that the pursuit of the satisfied, generous life must be achieved in the midst of our consumer-driven, debt-saturated culture. Do not think it will be a simple thing to extricate yourself from the trap of comparison.

No matter what you receive, buy, or achieve, you will soon encounter someone who has something newer, bigger, or nicer—a more generous expense account, a faster car, or a larger yacht. A more expensive home or an expansive corner office. A nicer set of golf clubs, a larger TV screen, or a better tan. Living by comparison will inevitably lead you to focus on what you lack rather than on what you have. Fixating on the blessings withheld may cause you to despise the marvelous blessings you possess.

What's in Your Bowl?

So what's in *your* ice cream bowl? Not the bowl of the family living down the street or the coworker in the cubicle down the aisle. Not the bowls of friends at church. Not your sister-in-law's bowl, and for goodness' sake, not the bowls of the well-dressed, wrinkle-free models who grace the advertising pages of magazines—these perfect people are a fiction. What's in *your* bowl?

Before reading another page, pause for a few moments and answer that question. Make a list. Right now, before moving on, simply itemize those blessings for which you can be deeply grateful. Do you have access to a public park or a library? Is there a friend you can call if you are deeply discouraged? Mention friends by name as well as beloved family members. List abilities you possess, not overlooking magnificent gifts such as literacy. Include health, the ability to work, and eyesight. Include physical blessings such as meals, clothing, and transportation. Did you eat yesterday? Are you likely to eat tomorrow? Your list should not be short.

Go ahead. What's in your bowl? Reflect for a few minutes right now and physically jot these things down. This act should be an exercise in gratitude, prompting an excursion into the land of the deeply thankful. Is your bowl overflowing? Does the action of scribbling this list make you feel, well, rich? It is from this vantage point that generosity thrives. When you calculate the goodness of God in your life, a giving spirit is unleashed.

Emptied

I am confident, though, that many of you attempting this exercise feel as if your bowl, once full, is now empty. As you read these words, your heart is awash with grief. Extended unemployment has wrecked you financially. The cancer is back. A child has broken your heart. An unbroken chain of disappointments has you feeling isolated and abandoned. The marriage you fought so hard to save was lost. Quite frankly, it feels as if your bowl has been turned upside down and emptied out.

I need you to do something. If your bowl has been emptied, flip it back over and look inside. Is it possible that God is still there? Is it possible that when our bowl is emptied out and the things upon which we relied are torn away, we can still experience his presence and his care and his friendship? Are you open to the prospect that it is possible to experience the presence and goodness of God more profoundly when our hearts are broken and our lives interrupted? What if our Father, Creator, and Healer is still there when all else is stripped away?

In dark times we may learn to love God for himself and not simply for his gifts. He's with you even when you get emptied out. He is with you and he is enough. He will never leave you. He will never forsake you.

PART 2: **Comparison**

Reflect and Discuss:

1. Can you think of an occasion when your satisfaction was crippled when you compared your situation with someone else's?

2. What are the dangers to our faith that come from a life marked by comparison?

Project: What's in your bowl?

Take some time and make a lengthy list of the blessings you are surrounded with. Find a quiet space to think through your life, and include not only physical items, but also relational, mental, and spiritual. Physical blessings: eyesight, hearing, mobility. Include various types of food and clothing, selecting individual items for which you are grateful. Include a list of friends.

Read back through your list. What does this experience do? Write your response or share your reflections with your small group.

PART 3

Identity Shift

08

Adopted

Identity Theft

I ran into Tony at the fortieth birthday party of a mutual friend. The party was hosted at a gorgeous home, and guests mingled on the spacious patio overlooking the manicured lawn and pool. It was a beautiful setting for a midsummer gathering.

Tony and I had not connected in years though we attended college together and live in the same city, and we welcomed the opportunity to catch up on each other's lives. Our small talk quickly moved through the usual paces, sharing about work, children, and what we'd been up to recently. But then it took one of those rare and refreshing turns toward honest vulnerability. Tony confided that he and his wife, Karen, were suffocating beneath a weight of financial pressure. This was not simply a temporary setback; they faced the very real prospect of financial ruin.

The number of guests milling about made the patio an awkward atmosphere for such an intimate conversation, yet

I felt his brutal honesty welcomed further dialogue. When I asked if he was interested in continuing our conversation over coffee, he seemed eager to talk. I suspect he had been carrying this weight for some time and was relieved to unburden himself in trusted company.

The following Monday morning we met at a downtown Starbucks a block from Tony's office. Thankfully, we had the outdoor seating area to ourselves and could converse freely and without interruption.

As Tony chronicled the financial drama they were facing, it became clear that adequate income was not the problem. Both Tony and Karen were employed and earning strong salaries. The issue, as Tony explained it, was an inability to keep spending under control. Tony confessed that the responsibility for runaway spending was overwhelmingly his fault. He felt an urgent, inner compulsion to keep up the appearance of someone who is well off. This compulsion drove not only his choice of a home but what kind of vehicles they leased, their expensive taste in clothing and restaurants, their decision to purchase a summer cottage, their desire for a country club membership, and plans for costly vacations. The sum of these commitments was enough to capsize their financial stability.

Tony had amazing clarity as to what was driving his consumptive lifestyle. He described a childhood of scarcity, shortage, and embarrassment. His father moved out when he was six, leaving his mother to support three children on an income that fell below the poverty line. One of Tony's most painful memories was being mocked by other kids in seventh grade for wearing pants that were way too short. He had experienced a growth spurt over the summer, and there was no money available to purchase clothing for the new school year. The ridicule took the form of that well-worn joke that Tony's pants were so high because he was preparing for a flood. This in turn led to the shorthand nickname "Flood" (or in some cases "Noah") — a moniker he wore throughout middle school, even after better-fitting clothes were purchased.

There were other memories — an empty refrigerator, subsidized school lunches, and his mother's constant fretting about overdue bills. But the laughter he endured over the short pants left the most indelible mark. Reliving the experience made it difficult for him to even make eye contact. As Tony shared these reflections, he stared down at his espresso cup, which rested on the table between us. Shame has a long memory.

As a seventh grader, Tony made a silent, determined vow that he would never, *ever* look poor again. Now sitting in front of me was a fairly successful forty-three-year-old man, strained to the breaking point financially in an attempt to fulfill that vow. Every purchasing choice was calculated to make an impression. But it seemed that no matter how much money they earned, it wasn't enough to compensate for the humiliation that had etched itself into his identity.

As we talked at the coffee shop that beautiful July morning, it was obvious that Tony's money crisis was the result of an identity crisis. The grown man sitting across from me in a smart business suit drinking espresso had scripted his lifestyle to outrun a childhood nickname: *Flood.*

Though Tony had a great deal of clarity on what was driving his spending, he seemed powerless to alter his compulsive behavior. Keeping up the appearance of wealth had become so central to his sense of self that not spending was like not breathing. To delay a purchase felt a bit like drowning. His identity, his life, depended on it.

For Tony—as for many of us—transforming the way he views spending, saving, and giving will require a transformation in the way he views his core identity. For the Christian, the issue of identity cannot be overestimated, for it is new identity that propels new behavior. Embracing our new identity has the power to draw us into a new and compelling narrative.

Belonging and Behaving

Let's explore the topic of identity by returning to Ephesus. The spectacular ruins of the site speak to the city's rich culture and vibrant economy. It is to this strategic city that the apostle Paul traveled on his third journey with the goal of establishing a community of Jesus followers. Paul spent almost three years in Ephesus—longer than he ministered in any other location. A few years after departing the city, probably writing from prison in Rome, Paul corresponded with believers in the region to further cultivate their growing faith. In the New Testament, we know this correspondence as the book of Ephesians.

I find it noteworthy that of all the subjects Paul needed to communicate with them about, he chose first to address the topic of identity. This intrigues me because so much in these new believers needed correcting. In chapter 4 of Ephesians, Paul turns his focus to behavioral issues such as lying, theft, bitterness, rage, slander, and malice (4:25–31). In chapter 5 he turns his attention toward sexual purity, greed, and intoxication (5:3, 5, 18).

Now, mind you, this letter was written to church people. It seems that there was a lot going wrong and new habits needed to be encouraged. But those words of correction could wait until the second half of his letter. Instead of launching into their behavioral struggles, Paul begins by focusing exclusively on the new identity of the Jesus follower. He seems intent on anchoring them in their sense of belonging. It's as if he says, "Before I remind you how to behave, I need to remind you that you belong."

In the opening sentences of Ephesians, Paul employs the three images of adoption, redemption, and sealing to convey the reality of our true identity. These concepts were crucial as

I sat with Tony that summer day at Starbucks, talking about appearances, overspending, and childhood nicknames. It is from a conscious decision to live out of our new identity, our sense of belonging, that true life-change is possible.

Adoption

Listen in as Paul opens his letter to his Ephesian friends.

> In love he predestined us for adoption to sonship through Jesus Christ, in accordance with his pleasure and will—to the praise of his glorious grace, which he has freely given us in the One he loves. (Ephesians 1:4–6)

The first image Paul uses to capture the identity of the one who has come to know and follow Jesus is adoption. This imagery intensifies when we travel back to the Roman world where child abandonment was common.

Let's take in a play together. The columned street originating at the harbor of Ephesus leads to the great theater with capacity for over twenty-five thousand spectators. The stage building rises three stories, graced with an elaborately ornamented façade. See the massive theater filling with spectators as we enter through a large vaulted entryway and locate our seats. The drama to be enacted on the stage below is the famous play *Oedipus Rex*. The tragedy is based on a well-known Greek legend:

King Laius and Queen Jocasta of Thebes receive a disturbing oracle that their newborn baby boy will cause the family grave harm. After Laius pins the infant's feet together, he directs his wife to kill the child. Jocasta, in turn, delegates the task to a servant. But instead the servant abandons the vulnerable baby in the fields, exposing the infant to the elements — leaving his fate to the gods. A shepherd finds the infant and names him Oedipus (swollen feet). The child is eventually raised by Polybus, king of Corinth.

This backstory is well-known to the thousands of theatergoers seated around you, who ready themselves for the performance.

Now, to that ghastly little background detail about the unwanted Oedipus being abandoned in the field, leaving his fate to the gods. No one seated in the theater of Ephesus finds this development of the storyline of the play unusual because exposing a rejected child to the elements is such a common practice. In Roman culture, a newborn is frequently placed at the father's feet. If the father wants to keep the baby, he picks it up, claiming it as a desired child. But the father may also disown the baby for any reason, in which case he simply turns his back and walks away. Perhaps he desires a boy and this is a girl. Perhaps he prefers a daughter and this is a son. Perhaps he detects some blemish — say, a birthmark — of which he disapproves. All the father has to do to reject the child is walk away. The rejected infant is then commonly placed outside, exposed to the summer heat or winter rains, to die of dehydration or hypothermia.

In Ephesus, it would not have been uncommon to pass the marketplace or the city garbage dump at night and hear the frail cries of babies who had been abandoned there. Speculators would frequently pick over the infants, evaluating them to discern whether they were likely to become strong and healthy. They might then "rescue the baby," most commonly for the purpose of raising the child to be sold later as a slave or prostitute. A few decades after Paul's stay in the city, the Ephesus doctor Soranus authored a manual titled, *How to Recognize the Newborn That Is Worth Rearing*. The booklet provided criteria for evaluating infants to determine the likelihood of their growing to be healthy and strong. The resource helped you discern whether raising this child promised a good return on investment.

I wonder how many young slaves scanned faces in the crowd while walking through the busy streets of Ephesus, wondering, "Is one of these men my father? Is one of these women my mother?" As the Jesus movement spread in Ephesus, it is certain that among the slaves who had become followers of the Christ, there were those who had been dumped as children, placed on the garbage heap, abandoned in the cold.

And to these Christians living in a culture of abandonment, Paul writes of the wonder of adoption. He begins his letter by reminding them that they have been adopted by the creator of the universe, that because of Jesus they have a treasured place in God's family. Before Paul gives any instruction on how to reform their lives or change their habits, he simply reminds them who they are. Before he encourages them to behave, he simply reminds them that they belong. They share a new identity as the community of the adopted.

> In love he predestined us for adoption to sonship through Jesus Christ. (Ephesians 1:4–5)

How did these words impact those who had been dumped as infants? As these words were read to Ephesian Christians, did some weep openly at being reminded that God adopted them? What was it like for them to grasp that their fundamental identity was no longer determined by the father who tossed them out but by the God who took them in?

This is the power of identity in Christ. This gift was not only revolutionary for Christians in first-century Ephesus; it has profound ramifications for believers today. Your new identity through God's adoption means that your most defining reality is not who abandoned, betrayed, or deserted you, however painful and scarring those events were. Your identity is not defined by the fiancé who broke off the engagement, the company that canned you, the parent who left you, or the spouse who betrayed you. Your most defining moment is not determined by who threw you out but who took you in. The

God of creation adopted you. He picked you out, he picked you up, he brought you home.

Our understanding of God's adoption has the power to transform every facet of life. Specifically, there is a strong connection between our identity and the way we view our belongings. I have a strong suspicion that many of us attempt to heal the wounds of the past by overfilling our already-full homes.

09

Bought

A Beautiful Day in the Neighborhood

Fred Rogers, the late ordained Presbyterian minister and host of the enduring children's television program *Mister Rogers' Neighborhood*, which ran from 1968 to 2001, articulated the inability of a purchase to meet deep, human need. Listen carefully to his wise words (from his book *The World According to Mr. Rogers: Important Things to Remember*):

> "The older I get the more I come to understand that the things we possess can never bring us ultimate happiness. Contrary to what is implied in the commercials, nothing we buy can take away our loneliness, fill our emptiness, or heal our brokenness."

Read these last words out loud—but in first person. Hear yourself say them.

> "Nothing I buy can take away my loneliness, fill my emptiness, or heal my brokenness."

The fact that our gracious God longs to be our Father is

intended to affect the way we spend, borrow, and give. Our new identity speaks into the incessant "wanting" that seems to permeate the very air we breathe.

If you have truly come to know Jesus, your most defining reality is not who dumped you but who adopted you. Receive these words: "The God of the universe picked you out, he picked you up, he brought you home." Identity as God's beloved sons and treasured daughters is the starting point for thinking clearly about who we are, what we have, and what we want. Identity is your starting point in calculating your abundance. Your new identity in Christ frees you to enjoy material blessings without demanding that they fill a void they can never fill or heal a wound they were never designed to heal.

Redemption

A new identity as someone loved and adopted is an incredible starting point for living the satisfied, generous life. But Paul isn't finished. After writing about the wonder of adoption, he continues to ground the Ephesian Christians in their identity by borrowing a term from the marketplace: *redemption*.

> In him we have *redemption* through his blood, the forgiveness of sins, in accordance with the riches of God's grace that he lavished on us. (Ephesians 1:7–8)

To redeem something is to pay for it. To buy it. When applied to people, the sense is that the person is released or ransomed as a result of being purchased.

Let's explore Paul's imagery of redemption by strolling to the main shopping district of Ephesus. We leave the theater and take a short walk up the marble street to the commercial marketplace. The massive market is the epicenter of commerce, not only of the city but for the entire region. An endless stream of products flows through this space; spices, clothing, and jewelry are all available for sale. But in this metropolis, you can also purchase people. In this first century, Ephesus is the world capital of the slave trade.

Imagine a slave working in an orchard. He has little decision-making power of his own. Every aspect of life is dictated by his owner. As he and the others work away pruning fruit trees, the foreman of the estate enters the orchard and yells his name. "Your owner wants to see you immediately," he barks. The other workers cast worried glances his direction, wondering what trouble awaits him on the other side of that summons. As he makes his way tentatively through the orchard and up the stone-paved path to the house, he scours his memory for any infraction for which he might be punished. But as he enters the courtyard, he observes not only his owner but also his own brother-in-law, whom he has not seen in four years. The brother-in-law has a small leather money bag in his open palm and audibly counts out coins, placing them on a tabletop—"Nineteen, twenty, twenty-one ..." The owner recounts the silver pieces, silently signs a document, and gruffly hands it to the brother-in-law. For the first time the relative addresses the slave. "Let's go home," he says as he smiles and motions toward the door. The slave exits the estate into a new life. His freedom has been purchased. He has been bought. Redeemed.

When Paul reminded these young Christians that they had redemption "through his blood" (Jesus' voluntary crucifixion), he was marveling that God's mercy stretched so far, that Jesus gave himself to pay for them. When Jesus paid for us to be released from the stranglehold of our trespasses, he did not fork over money but paid with his own life.

Paul remarked that our purchase is "in accordance with the riches of God's grace." Here he is announcing that Jesus' self-sacrifice, which buys us out of slavery, is exactly the kind of thing God would do. Our redemption floods from a God who is grace-rich. It's just what he does. He loves and he gives. The rescue mission God launched on our behalf flows from his generous heart.

Not only did he adopt you; he paid for your release. He adopted you and he bought you. Reflect on this reality the next time you begin to believe the lie that a material purchase you make will complete you.

Walk-In Closet

For several minutes Mindy stands peering into her walk-in closet. It is full. Packed. Every hanger used, every shelf occupied. As she scans her stockpile of clothing she mutters, "I don't have anything to wear." Realizing the irony, she considers that every item in this closet was liked at one point—at least when it was purchased. Liked enough to try it on in a fitting room, carry it to the checkout counter, and exchange money for it. It strikes her as mildly humorous that she loves everything she buys but little that she owns. In a more contemplative moment she muses, "Why do I shop when I am lonely, bored, or depressed?" Mindy has yet to ask the big question: "What if the empty space I'm attempting to fill isn't my closet?"

What does this story of the walk-in closet trigger in your thinking? We are inundated by advertisements that plead for our attention and dollars. One way or another, the commercial makes a promise: "Buy me and I will complete you." Do we crave reminders that expose this for the lie we know it to be? Do you long to be reminded that your worth is fixed in something more enduring than your latest purchase? Meanwhile, the words of our Christ—"Let anyone who is thirsty come to me and drink" (John 7:37)—beckon us to shun flimsy substitutes and quench our thirst in the clear running stream of Life.

When a potential purchase or compelling commercial whispers "Buy me and you will be whole," you can whisper back, "My identity does not depend on what I buy. My identity rests in who bought me."

10

Sealed

The Mark of Ownership

It is a Sunday morning in Ephesus. Having no church building, a group of believers is meeting in the courtyard of a large home. The gathering is comprised of a diverse cross section of the city. Ethnically, there are Jews and Gentiles. Economically, there are slaves and slave owners. Vocationally, there are tentmakers, silversmiths, dealers in cloth and cosmetics. This is your first visit to the community, and you strike up a conversation with a slave named Erastus. On his hand there is a tattoo—the emblem of his owner. The tattoo is the seal of ownership identifying the estate and family to whom this slave belongs.

The informal service includes singing sacred songs and a meal during which there is a pause to remember Jesus' sacrifice as bread and wine are shared. Then a segment of Paul's letter is read.

And you also were included in Christ when you heard the message of truth, the gospel of your salvation. When

you believed, you were marked in him with a seal, the
promised Holy Spirit.   (Ephesians 1:13)

The effect of the reading is stunning. A slave girl in the
group is deeply moved by the words. God has placed *his seal*
on her life, marking her as one who belongs to him. What if
her most identifying marker is not the tattoo on her hand but
the Holy Spirit in her heart?

When you came to believe in God's life-saving gift of the
cross, when you responded to the news that God showers
goodness on radically flawed rebels, he placed his seal of ownership on you by sending his Spirit to live inside you. You
belong to him now. You're his. He is yours and you are his.

There are days we simply need to remember whose we
are. Enjoy your house and yard. Enjoy a home-cooked meal
with friends. Enjoy the clothes that make you feel comfortable. Be thankful for the car or bike or pair of shoes or bus
that carries you to work. But remember, please remember,
that your identity is not anchored in *what belongs to you*. Your
identity is anchored in *who you belong to*. You are his. It's not
what you purchase. It's *who purchased you* that forms the core
of who you are.

As a Christian, I don't *get* my identity from my car. I *bring*
my identity to my car. I don't get an identity from my house.
I bring my identity to my house. I don't get my identity from
my career. I bring my identity to my career. My identity is
anchored in *who* I belong to, not *what* belongs to me.

Adoption. Redemption. Sealing. He adopted you. He bought you. You're his.

Blindsided

In his book *The Blind Side*, Michael Lewis chronicles the distressed upbringing of professional football player Michael Oher. One of thirteen children in Memphis, Tennessee, Michael was in and out of the foster care system from age seven. As his mom battled alcohol and crack addictions, his survival was so tenuous that he often had to "forage" for food and clothing, scrounging and scavenging whatever he could find. During much of his adolescent years he was functionally homeless, living with various acquaintances for a day or two at a time.

Academic challenges appeared insurmountable due to the instability of his life. During one stretch, Michael attended eleven different schools during a nine-year span. The Michael Oher story took a radical turn, however, when he began attending Briarcrest Christian School and was taken in by Sean and Leigh Anne Tuohy, an affluent couple whose children attended the same school. In time, the Tuohys adopted Michael.

Because Sean owned a chain of Taco Bell and KFC restaurants, the family could go to any of them and order whatever they desired—free of charge. When Michael came to live with the Tuohys, this luxury was extended to him. But when Michael visited one of the family's restaurants, he habitually ordered more food than he could eat, bringing home leftovers to stash in the fridge. This behavior was a result of his former encounter with hunger. His habit of hoarding revealed that he was still struggling with the concept that there was going to be enough to eat. Michael had a new home, a new security, a new family, and someone to call Mom and Dad. But he still battled old habits from his lengthy season of scarcity and shortage. Though he was surrounded with abundance, he inwardly believed that there was never going to be enough.

In a scene from the book, Sean describes Michael entering the house with an extra Mexican pizza, which would inevitably be left in the fridge to coagulate overnight. Michael would see Sean and go, "Oh, man, I forgot." He forgot he had a new home, a new security, a new family, and someone to call Mom and Dad.

Like Michael, we forget. We can forget that we have been adopted into a new life and a new home. Forgetting who we are, we too lose sight of our identity and our security.

The Journal

I journal faithfully. Not every day, but several times a week. I chronicle my joys, frustrations, major achievements, and lin-

gering disappointments. I scribble urgent prayers and nota-
tions of heartfelt gratitude. I chronicle the beauty of a winter's
day or the darkness of a depressive mood. It's the way I talk
to God. Writing out my prayers aids me in organizing garbled
emotions into articulate sentences.

And somewhere along the line, years ago and for reasons
I do not recall, I began signing off my daily entries with a
standard ending. After penning my thoughts and prayers and
hopes and rants, I generally close with these words to my
Lord: "This is Jeff, the son you love."

I don't write this to remind *God* who I am. I write this to
remind *me* who I am. I write this because I am prone to forget
that I am deeply loved by the Father. I remind myself that I
am his. He adopted me, paid for me, and I am his. I am his
cherished son. His treasured kid.

Somehow this identity speaks powerfully into who I am,
what I have, and what I want. It frees me to enjoy possessions
without attempting to find my identity through them. They
are nice but they shouldn't define me. I was reminded of this
truth as I sat with Tony at Starbucks that beautiful July day.
Our identity in Christ, knowing that we belong to him, serves
to remind us that material luxuries, status symbols, and clothing, houses, and cars are meant to be enjoyed but were never
given to stamp a sense of identity on our lives. Our gracious
Lord has already done that.

The Heidelberg Catechism opens with this question and answer:

Question: What is your only comfort in life and death?

Answer: That I am not my own, but belong with body and soul, both in life and in death, to my faithful Saviour Jesus Christ.

Adoption, redemption, and sealing. This is my comfort: that I belong! I belong to *him*. I belong to my faithful rescuer, Jesus Christ, who gave himself for me. This is my belonging and my identity. I am his and he is mine.

PART 3: Identity Shift

Reflect and Discuss:

1. What are common sources of identity for your friends and family? In your life, were there early life experiences that caused you to base your identity on what you owned or acquired?

2. How does a thorough understanding of our spiritual adoption, redemption, and sealing from Ephesians 1 influence your quest for contentment?

Project: The weeklong spending fast

Purchase nothing this week. This is a week to enjoy what you already own. Enjoy the clothing you already possess. Read books, listen to music, and view movies already in your possession. While we may consider food an exception, some will decide to eat what is already in their fridge and pantry. It might be possible to go the entire week without purchasing a single item.

What did you learn? Did this change anything about your week? Journal your thoughts, or share your reflections with your small group.

PART 4

The Challenge
of Affluence

11

Enjoy This

The Buffet

When our children were young, we drove cross-country to visit my grandparents in the small prairie town to which they had retired in Eastern Wyoming. Born in 1907, my aged grandfather had witnessed the massive technological changes of the twentieth century. Raised in Southern Illinois by a single mother attempting to provide for three children, Ernie endured extreme poverty. During the Great Depression he rode a boxcar to Colorado to search for work. While we loved the image of our adventurous grandfather sneaking aboard a train to seek out a better life, I think he remembered that trip as utterly desperate. My grandfather had experienced scarcity and shortage that I can only attempt to imagine.

One evening during our visit, Grandpa insisted on taking us out to dinner. So we loaded into our van and drove the thirty miles to a nearby town that boasted an "all-you-can-eat" buffet. As we traveled to our dining destination, Grandpa described the restaurant where we would be eating. "Now,

Jeff, the kids can go up for a piece of chicken. And when they finish, they can go back up for more. They can eat as much as they please." We drove a few more miles and my grandfather broke in again. "Now, they have pie at this restaurant, and the boys can go up and get a piece of pie. And when they're done with that piece of pie, they can get a second piece of pie. They can eat as much as they please." Upon arrival at the restaurant we were seated. Again, Ernie eagerly explained, "Now, the kids can select anything they want. And then, they can go up again." At this point I'm thinking, "Grandpa, thanks for breaking this down for me, but I understand how a buffet works."

Of course, it wasn't me who had trouble comprehending the concept of an all-you-can-eat buffet. It was my dear grandfather, who had lived his early childhood in such poverty. It was difficult for him to grasp that an eight-year-old could enter a restaurant and eat as much pie as he wanted. This experience was so alien to his own childhood that he was elated to offer the opulence of endless dessert to his great-grandchildren. But I was not raised in extreme poverty, and the wonder was lost on me, as it was lost on my children. The privilege of eating two pieces of pie felt … well, normal.

Solidly anchored in the middle class, most days I have to remind myself how rich I am. The remarkable gifts that surround me go unnoticed. They feel normal. I must confess that I am surrounded by luxury yet often immune to the wealth that separates me from former generations in America or from those in developing countries who gather sticks to bake over open fires, or walk miles to a community well, or are strangers to basic sanitation.

The tragedy is not that we who occupy the middle class are rich when compared to the larger world but that we are rich and utterly unaware. We are rich and forget that we are rich. The scandal is not how much we have but how little we think we have, and thus, how much more we expect and demand.

Our souls are in danger. In danger of the felony of ingratitude. In danger of straying from the God whose goodness is so immense and so often ignored.

The Houses on the Hill

Let's return to the ruins of Ephesus to recall the culture in which Paul and Timothy served.

As Paul trained Timothy, he urged him to give specialized guidance to the affluent segment of his congregation. The church apparently was comprised of a broad economic cross section, and the wealthy were singled out for special instruction.

Now, as tourists ascend Curetes Street, on a hillside just south of the vast marketplace, they pass the remains of what was once the high-rent district of Ephesus. The Terrace

Houses are now covered by a vast roof structure that protects the excavated remains of these elaborate homes. These were the houses of Ephesus's most prominent citizens, and it is here that the wealth of Ephesus comes into sharp focus.

The houses on the hill are located near the center of the city, conveniently situated near the agora, theater, baths, and library. A walk through the Terrace Houses reveals floors surfaced with elaborate mosaics of intricate geometric patterns artistically crafted with tens of thousands of small colored stones. The brick walls were first covered with plaster and then painted with murals. These colorful frescos depict scenes from theatrical plays and everyday life and bear portraits of

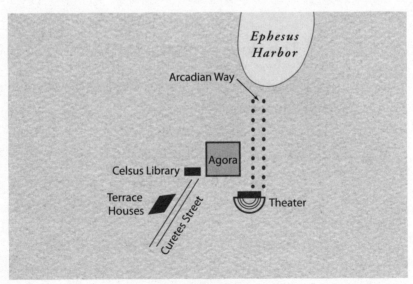

"Downtown" Ephesus.

philosophers and images of Greek gods and goddesses. No time or expense was spared in decorating these luxurious homes.

Furnaces not only provided hot water, but heated air for circulation through central heating systems. Clay pipes carried waste away from the lavatories to the main sewage system that ran beneath Curates Street. When excavating the site, archeologists discovered furniture and household objects made of bronze, ivory, and marble. The dwellings were designed for comfort and convenience. Welcome to the world of the financial elite of Ephesus.

Put yourself in the past and suppose that residents of the prosperous Terrace Houses area have become part of the Jesus community. What unique challenges will these wealthy believers experience in cultivating deep faith? What specific encouragement will they need to hear from their pastor? What unique barriers might their affluence pose? In short, how are these rich Christians to conduct themselves?

Press your ear to the first-century conversation and take these words to heart.

Paul advises Timothy:

> Command those who are rich in this present world not to be arrogant nor to put their hope in wealth, which is so uncertain, but to put their hope in God, who richly provides us with everything for our enjoyment.
>
> (1 Timothy 6:17)

I sense this is a significant teaching not only for the Ephesian wealthy but for our journey as well. It is important training for those of us who do not struggle to buy basic food items and who have sufficient clothing. It is for those of us who find ourselves immune to recognizing the luxury of an all-you-can-eat buffet. If we are wealthy—and by global standards most of us reading this are—how are we to conduct our lives and manage our wealth in a way that moves us toward our Lord rather than pushing us away from him?

Made for Our Enjoyment

Before we discuss Paul's encouragement about avoiding arrogance and before we explore his caution about putting our hope in wealth, focus for a moment on that last clause in 1 Timothy 6:17: God "richly provides us with everything for our *enjoyment*." The gracious Father provides innumerable gifts and wants you to enjoy them. Do these words surprise you? Imbedded in this guidance to wealthy Christians is a whispered invitation: "Enjoy this."

Could it be that the Creator designed, rigged, and crafted this world for our enjoyment? Observe some song lyrics with me. The poet who composed Psalm 104 raises a tune to the gracious, generous Creator. As you listen to the lyrics, immerse yourself in the vast goodness that surrounds us.

> He waters the mountains from his upper chambers;
>   the land is satisfied by the fruit of his work.
> He makes grass grow for the cattle,
>   and plants for people to cultivate—
>   bringing forth food from the earth:
> wine that gladdens human hearts,
>   oil to make their faces shine,
>   and bread that sustains their hearts.
>
>   (Psalm 104:13–15)

Drink in the rich imagery of the lyrics and the heart of gratitude lifted to the Giver who provides so lavishly. Rain falls and grain grows. Cows graze in fertile pastures. Vines yield clusters of grapes and trees produce abundant olives for oil. If you were to pen lyrics of gratitude for God's good gifts, what would you include? What daily enjoyments flood your life? From our world we enjoy bread and cheese. We dine on pasta accompanied by a glass of red wine. We savor the flavors of rich coffee, tangy oranges, tart apples, and crisp carrots. And he, the Creator, provides all this—intending for us to find his generous hand behind the dozens of enjoyments of each day and turn to him in gratitude.

As I write this, I sit on my backyard deck in the darkness. The area is illuminated by the flame of an outdoor fireplace. A small fountain gurgles a dozen feet away, augmenting the sounds of the summer evening with that of bubbling water. I smell the fresh bark spread in the flower garden below. It is a cool spring night, chilly enough to deter mosquitoes yet warm enough to sit outside—a truly glorious May evening. This night is a gift. In the simple luxuries of fountain and flame, I detect a whisper from my Lord: "Enjoy this." In this moment, I am deeply grateful. I feel blessed beyond anything I have done or deserve. All I can do is humbly receive this as a gift from the Giver.

Now here's my challenge: how to fall deeper in love with God and not my deck furniture. How to find my hope in God and not in my stuff. Will the enjoyment of these blessings stir or eclipse my affection for the Giver? I must humbly move toward receiving the gift of my backyard, the blessing of this wondrous evening, from the hand of a generous creator, but not hold God in contempt by loving his gifts more than I love him.

Pancake Dad

It's Saturday morning. Stan has determined to take the day fully off. No responding to emails from work, no repeatedly checking his phone for text messages. He stands at the stove flipping pancakes and frying eggs. Coffee brews. His wife sleeps in as his two pajama-clad, preschool sons watch cartoons in the adjacent family room. Mingled aromas fill the kitchen. He pours a mug of coffee and plates the pancakes and eggs as he calls his boys to the table. Stan's heart is full.

In this simple moment of cooking breakfast for his kids on an unrushed weekend morning, he is swept away by a wave of God's goodness. He feels rich. If he listens carefully in this moment, he will detect a whisper: "Enjoy this." As the boys scamper to the table, Stan breathes a response: "Thanks." This is worship—simple, pure, spontaneous gratitude to the Giver.

There have been other moments when Stan has felt this sensation. The previous summer things had been tight financially. One Sunday afternoon the family made an excursion to a county park twenty minutes from their home. The boys splashed in a shallow stream as he prepared a bed of coals on which to grill hot dogs. It was a postcard day—shade from massive oaks, warm but not oppressively hot. And laughter. Pure glee as his sons waded and splashed. A common adage proclaims that the best things in life are free. This expedition was not totally free but pretty close—the combined cost of dogs, buns, chips, and iced tea was around $10. But the richness of the day far exceeded the investment. Again, there was the whispered voice: "Enjoy this." And the responsive worship: "Thanks."

Do you hear his voice inviting you to enter into joy? The invitation calls to you as you sit beside a fireplace on a winter evening, or sip a steaming mug of tea, or view a bouquet of autumn trees. "Enjoy this." Hear the voice as you pick fresh vegetables from your garden, recline in the summer shade, enjoy morning espresso, or as your senses awaken to the scent of spring rain or crisp winter air. Respond to the goodness of the Creator with deep thanks and unbridled joy as you dig into a great salad, munch on a peanut butter sandwich, or share an unrushed dinner with friends. As you walk along the beach, hike beside a stream, or sit beside a fountain, open your heart to thank the Giver, who in Paul's words, "richly provides us with everything for our enjoyment." The pair of hiking boots, the warm jacket, the patio furniture and grill … Enjoy this.

12

The Power of Serving

A Life of Ease

We can easily grow oblivious to the riches that surround us, unmindful of the wealth in which we are immersed. Let me describe the opulence I encounter daily in my home. On winter mornings I awaken to a chilled house. I walk from my bedroom to the hallway thermostat. I turn the dial and warm air flows through my home. In fact, the furnace has kicked on from time to time throughout the night. Though chilly, our house is not frigid. This turning of a dial to generate heat is utterly amazing when you think about it—no shoveling coal into a furnace. No waking to a freezing home to kindle a fire. No stove to tend. No laborious cutting and splitting of wood. I turn a dial and my house warms. Amazing.

On a sweltering summer day, the twist of the same dial that brought warmth in the winter produces chilled conditioned air. Incredibly, inside my home it can be 70 degrees in both January and July.

Should I awaken before dawn, my sight obscured by the

darkness, I do not seek a match to light a lamp or candle. I throw a switch. With the upward motion of a one-inch lever, flipped with a single finger, light floods the room and darkness is expelled.

We do not wash our clothes by hand. We drop our stained garments into a machine and then pour in a bit of liquid detergent. We then turn a knob requiring a single twist of the wrist and a slight push. An hour later we return and find our clothing clean. We then throw it into another machine and return to find it dry.

The water that rushes into the washing machine? I do not draw it or fetch it. I do not walk to a town well or haul it to my dwelling from a spring. Nor do I wander into the backyard to pump water for the day's use. In both the kitchen and the bathrooms I turn a knob and clean water gushes forth. One knob for cold water and one for hot. We do not heat water for bathing. It issues forth from a shower head already heated.

Not having to first heat the water would make washing dishes by hand so much less laborious, but alas—we do not often wash our dishes by hand. The childhood argument following the evening meal over who will have to wash the dishes and who will get to dry them is but a memory from the past. We place the dishes in an automatic dishwasher, pour in a bit of detergent, push two buttons, and return a while later to discover them clean and dry.

What am I to say of the luxury of a flush toilet, a refrigerator, a microwave, an automobile, and email? And to what should I liken flight? I wait at the airport gate feeling perturbed at a forty-five-minute delay. Three hours later, I fly over Nebraska, looking to the distant ground below where wagon trains once churned up dust on their half-year journey from Missouri to Oregon. Basic antibiotics are offered at a cheap price at an area pharmacy. A century ago, what would a family have sacrificed to secure such medicinal magic as their child wasted away from an illness now easily cured?

Where Is Your Hope?

I am rich, yet frequently oblivious to my wealth. What would my Lord whisper into my opulent life?

Let's turn the corner and ask a penetrating question. How do the things you possess, the symbols of your success, affect your attitude toward yourself? Do your possessions lead to humble gratitude toward the Giver, or do you detect ego inflation as your financial profile grows?

Now we return to the first part of 1 Timothy 6:17, which we momentarily skipped over. "Command those who are rich in this present world not to be arrogant, nor to put their hope in wealth, which is so uncertain."

Why does Paul raise this issue? Why does he advise Timothy to warn against arrogance? Why was this warning needed in Ephesus, and why do we need this reminder so badly today? I suspect that our natural inclination — our gravitational pull — is to drift toward arrogance as wealth increases.

Wealthy believers in Ephesus were coached to flee arrogance. Conceit naturally and easily follows financial success, and it is vital to guard our hearts against it. If you work hard, advance in your career, and build wealth, there are several positive emotions you should experience. As you achieve, legitimate godly emotions might include deep satisfaction, gratitude, joy, and thanksgiving. But arrogant pride is an anti-God state of mind that corrodes the soul.

In verse 17, Timothy is also counseled to encourage the Ephesian affluent not to "put their hope in wealth ... but to put their hope in God." To put our hope in wealth is to depend upon it as our ultimate source of security. Only God should occupy this treasured position in our lives. With this admonition we return to the topic of core identity. In a consumer-driven culture, we are over-impressed by symbols of wealth. We need to remind ourselves again and again, "I make my money, my money doesn't make me. As a Jesus follower, it's not what I possess, but who possesses me that forms the core of my being. I earn money, spend money, and save money, but it will fail me if I place my hope in it. It is not my life and must not become my God."

The Creator reasons, "Don't put your hope in your stuff. Put your hope in me, the one who provides such things for your enjoyment." This generosity, this "rich provision," is designed to draw your heart home. It should cause deep sadness when we discover that the very gifts intended to draw our hearts to God result instead in egocentric pride. I think this will be the challenge of a lifetime: how to enjoy our possessions without placing our hope in them.

You won't have to work at becoming arrogant. As your wealth grows, just do nothing, and you will drift toward egotistical self-centeredness. It requires corrective action to prevent drift toward conceit.

The Lifestyle of Gratitude

What activities train the heart in humble gratitude? Are there disciplines that work to purge arrogance from our lives? Let's return to Paul's counsel to Timothy with regard to the financial elite of Ephesus—those who had the capacity to live in the houses on the terraces with elaborate floor mosaics and brilliantly colored wall frescos. When residents with this financial abundance became followers of the Christ, what could they do—and what can we do—to draw nearer to a true view of themselves, their wealth, and their God?

What Paul advises his protégé should not come as a surprise to us. He counsels Timothy to urge the wealthy to give themselves away, to be generous with their time and money. He challenges them, and us, to serve and share. Read this life-giving advice slowly and reflectively.

Command them {the rich} to do good, to be rich in good deeds, and to be generous and willing to share. In this way they will lay up treasure for themselves as a firm foundation for the coming age, so that they may take hold of the life that is truly life. (1 Timothy 6:18–19)

The first two pursuits (do good and be rich in good deeds) relate to the generous use of our time and may be combined under the heading "serving." The latter two pursuits (be generous and willing to share) relate to the generous use of our money and possessions and may be combined under the heading "sharing."

These endeavors reverse the pull of arrogance. Serving and sharing are two disciplines that counterbalance the potentially lethal effects of growing wealth.

Rich in Goodness: Serving

Paul encourages the affluent to serve (to do good and be rich in good deeds). But what does this have to do with money or arrogance? Think about it this way. The darker side to prosperity whispers, "It's all about you." Conversely, there is something about humble servanthood that trains the heart to answer, "No. It's *not* all about me." Serving is an un-self-centered state of mind. Done repeatedly, it forms an "others-focused" perspective. Serving as a way of life rescues me from the delusion that I am the center of the universe. As I devote my life to the discipline of doing good, I train my heart to confess again and again, "It's not about me." In this way, serving can work to combat the potentially narcotic effects of wealth.

So if you find your heart increasingly captured by money, then I have a suggestion. Serve routinely in your church nursery or volunteer faithfully at a veteran's facility. Visit a nursing home regularly, even if your consistency goes unnoticed and seemingly unrewarded. If you discern that growing wealth has become your obsession, teach a third-grade Sunday school class or take meals to families with newborns. Sign up to clean the church during the week or regularly mow the lawn for your cranky, elderly neighbor.

I think the idea here is that we are prone to spend a considerable amount of time thinking about ourselves. The remedy is not attempting to think of yourself less but to think of others more. As I focus more on serving others, less of my heart space is available to obsess over my bank account or my next purchase. My mind is using that energy to plot the welfare of others. I think this is why Paul advises wealthy Christians to devote themselves to lives of service. Serving purges the heart of arrogance that is the common by-product of affluence.

Do Something

A word of caution before departing from this topic: The affluent believers in Ephesus were encouraged to "do good." This
encouragement feels unarguable. But consider for a moment
that to do something good you actually have to *do* something.
This idea of doing good is not *thinking* about doing something
good, or *raising awareness* about doing something good, or
offering to do something good. It is actually *doing* good.

I find myself with a grieving friend at a funeral home vis-
itation. The weight of the loss is suffocating and the journey of grief will be long. We stand there together, and I offer
with utmost sincerity, "If you need *anything*, call me." And I
mean it. With these truly heartfelt words, I have just offered
everything but not yet done anything. I have now handed my
friend a blank check, but it is neither dated nor signed.

Such an offer places two obligations on the recipient. The
person who is grieving, or depressed, or exhausted has now
been dealt twin responsibilities: (1) They must ask for my
help. (2) They must be creative enough to know what it is
they need. But my experience is that people in extreme pain
or confusion often lack the willingness to ask for help, even
if they have the creativity and clarity to discern what to specifically ask for.

I suggest that doing *something* is often better than promising *everything*. The simple act of scribbling a note on a

restaurant napkin to say "I'm thinking of you today; you're not alone" and then handing it to someone may be of greater comfort than notifying them of our availability should they desire to ask for it.

Also, those simple ways we might help out—almost effortlessly—feel weighty when the request is placed on the shoulders of the hurting person. Consider a common act of goodness: Jane's isolated friend struggles with an onslaught of postpartum depression following the birth of her third child. Jane calls her to announce that on the way home from work she will pick up a pizza and drop by for a few minutes. With this simple gesture, she gives the dual blessings of thirty minutes of companionship and a simple meal her fatigued friend will now enjoy without needing to prepare it. What will this gift cost Jane? Perhaps $18 and half an hour—almost nothing to bless her discouraged, conversation-starved sister. But flip the scenario around. Now place the burden of responsibility on the new mom. Imagine her dialing Jane's number and requesting, "When you leave the office today, could you please buy a pizza for us, and then come to the house and listen to me talk for half an hour?" What was a relatively simple act of goodness when offered would seem monumental to request. It is unlikely that this mother will have the nerve to ask, but more than that, she may be in an emotional condition where she can't discern how such a gift, how simple food and conversation could lift her day.

So rather than offering everything, do something. Do anything. Place the responsibility upon yourself. Be creative and offer something specific. If your offer meets a genuine need, then follow through. The life of goodness requires initiative and motion. "Command them to do good, to be rich in good deeds" (1 Timothy 6:18). This was Paul's encouragement through Timothy to wealthy believers in Ephesus, who ran the risk of growing self-absorbed. He challenges them—and us—to lives of humble service. Though this service can be a significant source of help to others, it also changes *you*. Don't underestimate the ability of gracious, humble service to shape your attitudes toward yourself and others.

Another word before pressing on: I have discovered a major barrier to "doing good." It is, quite naturally, our belief that "doing good" is not good enough. We don't want merely to do something *good*. We want to change the world. We aspire to do something *great*. Our desire is to live *great* lives and have a *great* impact, so we look for *great* things to do. As we keep a sharp eye out for "great things" to come along, we wait. We wait as we attempt to identify our unique contribution to the human race. We wait for some massive breakthrough moment. We wait to be discovered. And as we are waiting to do something great, a parade of opportunities to simply and humbly do something good goes marching by. While waiting for one moment of greatness, we miss out on a thousand moments of goodness.

Here's a thought: What if we led great lives not by doing great things but by doing good things over and over and over again. What if the path to greatness is repetitive goodness? What if greatness is goodness compounded? I suspect that we arrive at greatness through the lengthy corridor of repeated, small, humble acts of goodness.

Does Paul's advice sound strange to you? In his encouragement to the wealthy, we might expect him to talk about greed, but instead he advises the course of servanthood. Do not underestimate the power of a life of service to retrain the channels of the heart. A life dedicated to small acts of serving others leads us away from a life of self-focused self-importance. I have come to believe that I will not defeat greed by focusing on greed. But perhaps I will deflate greed by focusing on serving. As acts of humble service compile, we begin to think of others more and about ourselves less. Subtly, slowly, materialism loses its death grip on our lives.

13

The Power of Sharing

Rich in Generosity: Sharing

While walking the shore of Lake Michigan during a weekend getaway, while relishing a rich cup of coffee with cream, or while enjoying an unhurried dinner on our deck with friends, something in my heart should resound with gratitude. Deep and pure thanks should emerge. As I hear the Creator whisper, "Enjoy this," a sincere question should arise from my heart: "In response to your goodness, is there anything you desire from me?" And my Lord will likely answer, "Yes, I want you to share."

In Timothy 6:18, Paul mentions an additional pair of disciplines that can train our hearts toward a proper view of our wealth. These behaviors relate to the activity of sharing. Timothy is advised to encourage the rich to "be generous and willing to share." It is not only our acts of service but also financial generosity that enables us to think sanely about who we are, what we have, and what we want. Generosity is at the core of the satisfied life.

This makes a lot of sense to me. One way to combat the grip money has on my heart is to consistently, faithfully, and generously give it away. The most anti-accumulation thing an affluent person can do is to systematically give money away. The discipline of giving frees my heart from a growing infatuation with my stuff. Giving is the natural outflow of the thankful heart. Sharing is living in step with a God whose heart is wildly generous.

Later

My encouragement is for you to act immediately and decisively in this area. When prompted by God to pursue generous giving, good-hearted Christians rarely say "no." I think a more common response is for us to say "later." What is lethal about this response is that we really mean it. Watch the journey of well-intentioned refusal:

"I really desire to become a person of deep generosity but just not now. I'm graduating from college encumbered by student loans. I'm applying for my first real job and just getting started in a career. Systematic, generous giving is something I fully intend to pursue ... but later."

And we mean it. And five years pass.

"I fully intend to manage my resources to serve my church in a significant way and alleviate suffering in the world—but later. We're newlyweds, saving for the down payment for our first home."

We don't say "no," we say "later," and we sincerely mean it.

But months become years, and now children toddle around the house and our spending is dominated by vehicles and vacations. Myriad voices compete for our dollars. "Later," we reason, and we mean it. But "later" keeps getting delayed. Those once small children are now college bound, and our retirement savings have not grown as anticipated. A day for generous giving will come, but it will have to be later.

And the well-intentioned disciple awakens to discover that decades have passed. And "later" actually meant "no."

This is why I earnestly challenge you to begin somewhere and begin now. Begin to give to your church today. Not merely fishing through your wallet to see what you can spare as the offering basket is being passed, but regular, budgeted, faithful giving. Begin today to set aside funds that can be routinely given away as you become aware of people in financial need or ministries that stir your heart.

Begin somewhere. Begin now. Do not postpone or procrastinate giving because you are waiting to "feel led" to give. Begin now based on the clarity God has already given. Do not fall victim to the deception of well-intentioned delay. Your life will pass you by and you will miss out on the adventure of giving.

It is not only our potential for good that is halted. My sense is that when we refuse to follow God's clear direction with regard to financial generosity, the refusal can stunt growth in every other area of our discipleship. Refusal to move forward in this region will paralyze our maturity. Conversely, when we respond to God's movement in this area, barriers to growth in other regions start to fall like dominos. Telling God "yes" and not "later" opens my spirit to follow my Lord. I find I am more likely to respond with a "yes" when I am prompted to offer forgiveness or offer an apology. I am more apt to respond obediently when nudged by God to step into a messy situation and offer comfort or encouragement.

So, you see, saying "yes" to God in the difficult arena of generosity opens my heart to following him in other areas. In this way, I believe that aggressive, systematic giving unleashes dynamic growth.

As you press your ear to the conversation between Paul and Timothy, also hear our Lord whisper into your life: "Enjoy the blessings I provide! Enjoy this. Don't try to find your hope in your stuff. As you enjoy my goodness, serve and share. Enjoy life, real life, as it was meant to be enjoyed."

PART 4: The Challenge of Affluence

Reflect and Discuss:

1. As affluent Christians, what unique threats does wealth pose to our faith?

2. How does serving others help us to fight against the arrogance caused by affluence? Similarly, how does giving help in this fight?

Project: Serve some place this week where you do not usually serve

Volunteer to clean up after an event at church or a local 5K charity race. Assist a neighbor with a cleaning project or help someone move. In this service opportunity, attempt to seek something that is low profile, for which you will not receive a lot of attention. Perhaps your serving opportunity could involve writing a long overdue note of thanks to a former coach, teacher, or youth pastor who impacted your life years ago.

Project: Calculate your annual giving

My suspicion is that we think ourselves more generous than we actually are. This week's project is about financial giving to your church, nonprofit organizations, or other types of charitable giving. Actually add up the amount you contributed last calendar year. What percentage of your total income was this?

You will not be asked to share any numbers with your group, but please be willing to share reflections. Did the exercise assist you in detecting anything about yourself?

PART 5

The Generous Heart

14

The Cycle of Care

The Adoption

Over dinner, Rick and Carla listen attentively as their friends, James and Lori, confide that rocketing costs may derail their dreams to adopt a second child. They offer sympathetic words, trusting their encouragement will show their love and care for their friends who so desperately want this child. The next day, however, an uninvited thought worms into Rick's mind: "We could help James and Lori cover the cost of the adoption." For some reason, this idea he would expect to be fleeting … doesn't flee. In the stream of random ideas that float through his mind that day, this particular impulse lodges, unwilling to drift away. The impulse feels stronger than simply a thought or idea. He wonders if this is what others refer to when they speak of receiving a "prompting" or a "leading" from God. Could this nagging idea, this impression, be a nudge from God?

Rick and Carla work diligently, even obsessively, to curb expenses and meticulously grow their savings. Rick loves to see their savings compound. A substantial gift would move their bank account in the wrong direction — backward. As he travels through a day overrun with sales meetings, emails, and phone calls, Rick finally manages to push the adoption from his mind. After all, they already give faithfully to their church and have their own financial goals to worry about.

Later that evening, Rick answers emails as a ball game is broadcast on TV. Carla enters the family room, picks up the remote, and presses mute. This gesture indicates that she wants Rick's complete and undivided attention. "I had a crazy thought today," Carla begins, tentatively. "A thought crossed my mind this morning. I think maybe we are supposed to help James and Lori pay for the adoption." Rick stares at her in disbelief for a moment before confessing that the same thought had lodged in his mind earlier in the day.

The fact that this strong impulse came to them both, but separately and independently, increases their suspicion that God may be moving them to help their friends make this adoption a reality. The ball game is turned off and they begin what could be a very expensive conversation. They realize that the check they are to write is not for a nominal amount. This will be the largest single gift they have ever given away. And with this gift their own financial goals will take a backseat; their savings will move in the wrong direction.

As Rick and Carla debate their role in funding the adoption, we need to recognize there is more than a check — more than money—in play here. Whenever we are prompted to give sacrificially and generously, something powerful is at stake. Whether a substantial gift to dear friends, or systematic, scheduled contributions to our church, giving is an exercise in trust.

At the center of biblical generosity lies the belief that God truly provides all that we need. With gratitude for what he has already provided, and confidence that he will continue to provide, we open our hands to release funds in a way that would honor our Creator. We enter a cycle of care, where God provides, we give, and God provides again. But if we are skeptical of God's goodness, if we are not confident of his care, a lifestyle of generous giving will almost certainly be short-circuited. For Rick and Carla, the decision to withdraw precious savings to assist their friends could mark a new chapter in their journey of trust.

Generosity Training

Be assured that we are not the first generation to wrestle with the challenge of generous giving. In the first century, new communities of Christians sprang up around the Mediterranean. These young believers needed solid training in the art of sacrificial giving. Let's travel to the Greek city of Corinth and witness the challenge of these early believers as they wrestled with an opportunity that required sacrifice and trust.

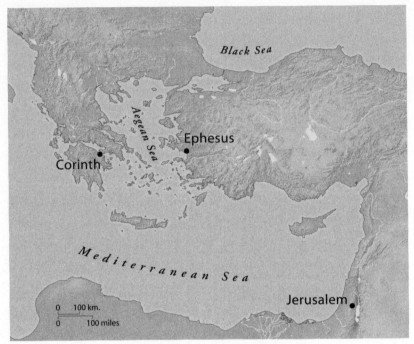

Corinth in relationship to Ephesus.

Across the Aegean Sea from Ephesus lies Corinth, located on the narrow sliver of land connecting the mainland of Greece with the Peloponnesian Peninsula to the south. Corinth is the most dominant commercial power in Greece because of its strategic location along the trade route between upper and lower Greece and the shipping opportunity made possible by its two harbors. Having been completely destroyed a century earlier in a conflict with Rome, the city is rising from the ashes with new building projects and construction.

Corinth is constantly in motion, a truly international city. When the apostle Paul visited during his second missionary journey, he earned his living manufacturing tents with a couple named Priscilla and Aquila. Shortly after Paul's departure, a leader named Apollos served the Corinthian church. What I find fascinating is that Paul was from Tarsus (modern-day Turkey), Priscilla and Aquila had recently arrived from Italy, and Apollos was from Alexandra, Egypt (see Acts 18–19). These four found their way to Corinth, not simply from different cities but from three different *continents*! I get the impression that such a thing is not unusual in Corinth. It is a multicultural city where you are likely to hear numerous languages and dialects as you stroll down its major streets.

Corinth is also famous as a sports destination. The Isthmian games, second only in popularity to the athletic contests in Olympia, are held every two years. Masses flock to Corinth to view the prestigious competitions in running, wrestling, boxing, discus, and javelin. I suspect that the athletic fanaticism in Greece was as intense as that of European soccer enthusiasts or diehard Green Bay Packers fans today.

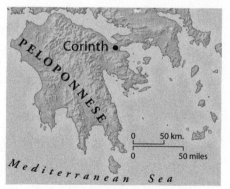

Corinth as Greece's strongest commercial city.

I write this not to turn you into encyclopedic experts on biblical cities but to show that in many ways, their world was not that different from ours. Corinth was highly mobile, extremely commercial, and sports crazed. Remembering this reduces the gap between their world and ours. I imagine that new Christians who called Corinth home must have struggled with generosity, just as we are likely to.

Promises, Promises

Paul spent a year and a half establishing a community of Jesus followers here. His visit is chronicled in Acts 18, and his correspondence to the young church is recorded in the New Testament letters of 1 and 2 Corinthians.

Embedded in Paul's second letter to the Corinthians are some of the Bible's strongest encouragements toward generous living. Earlier, Paul had challenged believers in the region to contribute to a famine relief offering to assist impoverished Christians in Judea (see 1 Corinthians 16:1–3). His hope was not simply to alleviate human suffering but also to unite the Jesus community. While the believers in Judea were predominantly Jewish, most of the Jesus followers in Greece were non-Jewish and had turned to Christ from their former lives of idol worship. The offering Paul asked for would provide needed food and clothing for fellow Christians, but it was also intended to bond followers who had come to Jesus from radically different backgrounds. Paul believed the offering was crucial in unifying two diverse segments of the church, and he poured enormous energy into the collection of these funds. This is why he is deeply troubled when the offering fails to materialize in Corinth.

When Paul first made his impassioned appeal for contributions to this offering, the Corinthian believers responded with enthusiasm, promising their strong, generous support. But their enthusiasm swiftly faded, prompting Paul to now offer much-needed coaching on the topic of giving. When he pens his letter addressing their lapse, instead of scolding, or pleading, or demanding that they follow through on their commitment, Paul patiently unfolds clear teaching on the topic of generous living. His words in 2 Corinthians, chapters 8 and 9, provide incredible guidance to anyone seeking generosity as a way of life.

The Provider

Paul reminds the Corinthian readers that as they engage in risky giving, their gracious God will provide all that they need and even beyond what they need. Read these words slowly and thoughtfully. Listen carefully. Meditate on their meaning.

Each of you should give what you have decided in your heart to give, not reluctantly or under compulsion, for

God loves a cheerful giver. And God is able to bless you abundantly, so that in all things at all times, having all that you need, you will abound in every good work.... Now he who supplies seed to the sower and bread for food will also supply and increase your store of seed and will enlarge the harvest of your righteousness. You will be enriched in every way so that you can be generous on every occasion, and through us your generosity will result in thanksgiving to God.   (2 Corinthians 9:7–8, 10–11)

As you read these verses, what concepts jumped out at you? Did you notice that these passages are anchored in the generosity of God? As we give, God graciously provides for us. When I read the words, "You will be enriched in every way so that you can be generous on every occasion," I'm struck that the intended end result of God's provision is not that we amass wealth or accumulate more stuff but that we continue to grow in goodness and generosity. This concept is also amplified in Paul's statement, "And God is able to bless you abundantly, so that ... you will abound in every good work." God's abundant blessing is to result in our expanding goodness. I believe this is what Paul means when he proclaims that God will "enlarge the harvest of your righteousness." God's blessing flows into my life so that it can flow out of my life.

When God blesses you financially, a normal and natural result should be increased giving. We are invited to participate in a God-driven cycle where we give, God responds with blessing, and we respond with increased, gratitude-driven giving. When we take care of God's interests, he takes care of us, so that we can continue to take care of his interests. If you are growing in income and not growing in giving, something has gone badly wrong.

But for the Corinthian church — and for most of us today — sacrificial giving unleashes a spiritual wrestling match. Remember the context of Paul's encouragement. The Corinthian believers had promised their strong support for the famine relief offering but then failed to follow through. I think it is common to be conflicted about giving. Something in our heart is moved toward generosity, and something in our heart resists it.

The Offering Basket

John sits near the back of the church he has grown to love. It's the midpoint of the service — the space between the singing and the sermon. In this intermission of sorts, a few announcements are given and the offering is collected. At Faith Community Church, offering baskets are passed down the aisles. This church isn't known for high-pressure tactics when it comes to the offering. Instead, from time to time, the person announcing the offering gently invites ...

"If you have begun to attend Faith Community regularly and have made this church your home, please consider giving in a systematic and generous way. We would appreciate your commitment so much, and we need your financial devotion to finance the ministry that means so much to so many."

John muses on the expression "systematic and generous." Week after week the offering basket passes by. And week after week John takes a mental inventory of the cash in his wallet. Perhaps a five or ten is plopped into the basket, a twenty on a charitable day. But systematic and generous? Hardly. And he loves this place.

Over the past three years he has transitioned from infrequent visitor to regular attendee. He is spiritually fed here — most weekends the sermon speaks into his life, guiding him, drawing him forward in his knowledge of Jesus and in his journey of faith. His eighth grader is involved in the youth ministry and his two grade-schoolers rave about the children's program. What a contrast to the memories of boredom attached to his own childhood church experience. Faith Community has deepened his faith and is reorienting his life around God-directed priorities. His wife, Beth, is currently enjoying a women's Bible study.

Three years. He can't believe it's been three years since the Easter Sunday when he and Beth first drove into the parking lot and nervously made their way into the auditorium. Now he sits, once again, at the midpoint of the service. The offering is announced, and he feels stirred, not simply to impulsively drop a larger bill into the basket but to reorient his financial world around this moment. He believes he is being moved, called, to contribute in a significant way. John feels a distinct prompting to transition from impulsive/nominal to systematic/generous. In a materialistic, consumer-driven world, this is a massive countercultural shift.

Witness the internal challenge going on in the back of the church. A battle ensues based on the simple reality that everything given away will no longer be John's to control, spend, or save. When money is given away, it is no longer available to place in his retirement fund, spend remodeling his kitchen, purchase basic necessities such as groceries or gas, or splurge on weekend getaways. Will John *have* enough and will he *be* enough if he takes this wild leap toward sacrificial giving to his church?

Don't underestimate the power of fear to hold you back from becoming the radically generous person you long to become. As you begin to dream about ordering your financial life around giving money away, sobering questions may arise:

What if that clunking sound from beneath my floorboard is my car demanding a new transmission?

What if two or three appliances in our fifteen-year-old home all decide to die at once? (I call this the "appliance alliance," where they meet secretly at night, collaborating on a simultaneous work stoppage.)

What if the stock market plummets again and my retirement savings falter with it?

If we decide to travel a few weeks from now, will giving restrict our plans?

As college tuition continues to climb, will we be in a financial position to assist our kids?

Fear of the future can paralyze the generosity of today. As John sits in the back of the church contemplating his commitment to giving, there is a voice that must prevail. He needs to hear his Lord's clear voice:

"Just look after my interests and I will look after you. Do what I'm asking you to do and I will meet your daily needs. I may also surprise you by blessing you with things far beyond your needs. But I need you to trust me in this adventure."

The Farmer's Field

To address this internal conflict as seen in 2 Corinthians 9:10, the apostle Paul borrowed farming imagery as a metaphor for giving. When he wrote, "He who supplies seed to the sower … will also supply and increase your store of seed," Paul was using planting and harvesting language.

Like the farmer who waves good-bye to his grain as it leaves his hand and disappears into the soil, as we give money away we can experience a sinking feeling that we are parting with something precious that we'll need. This question naturally arises: "If I give this away, am I certain I will have enough for me?" Like a nervous farmer, we can grow fearful that we won't have enough for our needs or for our comfort. But the Creator designed an agricultural system where seed thrown to the ground results in a harvest. This same creative, generative God can replenish my savings as I "throw" money to serve my church and care for people in need. The question is whether I can truly believe that God superintends a cycle of care. I believe our response will depend heavily on our confidence in the goodness of God.

Amazing Grace

When we approach this dangerous topic of sacrifice, it is essential to recall that our whole story as Christians is anchored in God's grace. To worship God for his grace is to marvel at the self-giving nature of God, to celebrate the overflow of his generosity. One of the first verses a child learns in Sunday school is John 3:16: "For God so loved the world that *he gave his one and only Son*" (emphasis added). God loves and he gives. This is his nature, his character to do so.

He was gloriously generous in the way he crafted our planet with color, and texture, and beauty. He is wondrously generous in the gift of his Son, who stood in as our substitute when he died for us. One of the most powerful expressions in Paul's treatise on generosity reminded the Corinthian reader—and reminds us—to go back to the beginning of our story, to begin not with our generosity but with the generosity of God. Paul reminds the young Christians in Corinth,

> For you know the grace of our Lord Jesus Christ, that though he was rich, yet for your sake he became poor, so that you through his poverty might become rich.
>
> (2 Corinthians 8:9)

Any generosity, sacrifice, or servanthood on my part is a reaction, a response to the generous Christ, who lavishly gave himself for me. Whenever we act with generous goodness—whether placing a sizable check in the church offering basket, financially sponsoring a child in a developing country, or supporting friends on a short-term mission trip—we can be certain that we are not making the first move. We are simply responding to the God who leads the way in giving. We are generous because we receive God's generosity in Christ. We forgive because he forgave. We love because he loved. We give because he gave. It is within our spiritual DNA to live as givers.

When you give generously, you reflect God the Creator, who embodies self-giving love. Perhaps the reason "God loves a cheerful giver" is that he himself gives generously, and when you mimic this trait, he is molding you into his character. Cheerful, generous givers reflect the Father.

15

Daily Bread

Childhood Stories

As a child, I was privileged to witness some pretty remarkable stories of God's provision. Right out of Bible college, my mom and dad moved to Southeast Idaho to begin a ministry planting churches. It was a pioneering ministry—attempting to grow a church community in a region with minimal Christian influence. They had virtually no funding, and they dealt with financial shortage on a regular basis. The words of the Lord's Prayer, "Give us today our daily bread," were not an abstraction to my mom and dad. They moved where they felt God had guided them to move, did the work they believed their Lord had directed them to do, and trusted that they would have what they needed, when they needed it. It was truly a faith venture, an adventure of trust. They experienced God's faithfulness again and again.

One of the more dramatic stories of God's provision occurred one day when my dad returned home from his office at the church to find my mother in tears. As I recall, it was the beginning of a new school year and mom had compiled a lengthy list of the immediate expenses she anticipated: school supplies, school clothes, medical costs, groceries, necessary household items — all things she felt we needed but could not afford. She had itemized these necessities and added up the amount required to cover them. The sum was $727. By today's standards, this may not feel like an astounding amount, but in the late '60s, on a miniscule income, it apparently felt overwhelming. In fact, the sum seemed so insurmountable that it was difficult to believe God would meet such a colossal need. As my dad relates the story today, he and my mom knelt and prayed. They had a strong belief that their Lord saw their needs and cared deeply for them. The prayer itself was a confession that God could provide what they needed in any creative way he chose.

Later that day, when Dad went to get the mail, a single letter awaited him at the post office. It was from a couple in California whom he knew by name but had never personally met. The letter was brief and said that they had recently sold a small business — a milk route from back in the day when milk was delivered by bottle to people's doorsteps — and the profit from the sale was $7,270. The letter went on to relate that they desired to give away one tenth of the amount they received from the sale and for some reason they had an impression that this should be sent to my parents. Enclosed in the envelope was a check for $727 — the exact amount my mother had cried over and that my parents had prayed over earlier in the day.

As far as I know, this is the only instance that a specific financial need was met for them to the exact dollar amount. But this event and others that were similar but less dramatic made a huge impact on me as a child. My mom and dad were faithful to relay these stories, and they made a strong impression upon my own faith development. In the early years of my life I was reared on stories of needed funds arriving from unexpected sources. I grew up believing that I was part of a system: If you looked out for God's interests, he looked after you. The stories my parents relayed prepared me for my own journey of trust. They groomed me for days when I needed to embrace God's leading and learn to depend on his provision.

Trust is a thread running through pages of our Bible. Specifically, we encounter the consistent theme of God's desire to be trusted in extreme situations. Though the Old Testament story of Elijah is not fundamentally a narrative about giving, it does provide a powerful example of radical trust and gracious provision that are foundation stones for the generous life. In retelling a segment of Elijah's story from 1 Kings, I hope to encourage those readers who are being called into a season of radical trust.

The Fugitive

Each day he drinks from the stream. Each day the water level recedes. Eventually, the stream will reduce to random puddles and then to a dry, rocky depression in the baking ravine. When that day arrives, he will seek a new place to hide. Elijah is a wanted man. But for now, he drinks from the stream and waits for his breakfast to arrive.

Drought bakes the land of Israel, scorching crops, cracking the earth, and propelling the people toward desperate ruin. Elijah is blamed for this famine because the parched ground is a direct result of his passionate prayer and prophetic voice. Elijah prayed for this drought. He called it down. This is why the hunted prophet hides in the Kerith Ravine, sipping water from the receding brook. Though blamed, Elijah is not responsible for the barren landscape. The devastation can be traced directly to a royal wedding.

To strengthen a political alliance with Phoenicia to the north, King Ahab of Israel married Jezebel. The new queen is an ardent evangelist for the fertility god, Baal, who is the deity credited for bringing agricultural abundance to the land. Jezebel believes fervently that it is Baal who blesses the land with abundant wheat, brimming vats of olive oil and wine, fig trees laden with fruit. Her fanaticism for Baal worship is absolute. To eliminate competition for her favored god, she systematically kills the prophets of Jehovah—the invisible, creator God of Israel—and under her ruthless reign Baal worship becomes the national religion. In the days of Ahab and Jezebel, spiritual confusion reigns. At dinner time, if you pass a village home at the end of a day's work, you can see a family enjoying bread dipped in olive oil, hear them offer a prayer of thanksgiving for the blessing of their meal: "Give thanks to Baal for he is good. His love endures forever." These are confusing times.

Elijah lifts his prayers to the heavens and his prophetic voice to the king. "If you trust in Baal to bring moisture to the earth, life and blessing to the land, then let's see what Baal can do. But by the name of Jehovah, the God of our fathers, whom I serve, there will be no rain. There will be no dew. Until I return and announce the end of this national disaster, the land will dry. The crops will die. The power of God will be revealed and the impotence of Baal will be exposed. This is the word of the Lord to Ahab and Jezebel." And with the delivery of this message to the king and queen, the word of the Lord comes to Elijah—"Run and hide!"

"Leave here, turn eastward and hide in the Kerith Ravine, east of the Jordan." (1 Kings 17:3)

With these words Elijah is driven into seclusion. But the Kerith Ravine boasts no grocery stores, no farmers' market. No farms for that matter. How will the man of God survive?

How does one subsist in such a remote place? The Lord broaches this topic in Elijah's deployment.

> You will drink from the brook, and I have directed *the ravens* to supply you with food there."
>
> (1 Kings 17:4, emphasis added)

As I read the story of Elijah's seclusion in the ravine, the whole episode spawns a litany of questions.

Did Elijah have any precedent for aviary catering?

Did Elijah have friends?

Did he tell them that he was headed to the middle of nowhere?

Did any of them venture to say, "Dude, you're going to starve to death."

Did Elijah tell them that he believed God would provide for him?

Did he reveal that he heard a voice informing him that ravens would deliver his food?

Did his family think him delusional?

Did they remind Elijah that ravens subsist on roadkill?

Did Elijah experience any flickers of doubt?

Is it possible, as he made his way over the cloudless landscape, across the Jordan River, and up into the ravine, that he muttered, "What the heck have I gotten myself into?"

We watch with awe as Elijah obeys. Whatever his doubts, fears, and apprehensions, he trusts God enough to travel to this secluded, un-peopled place. He runs and hides and God provides.

So he did what the *Lord* had told him. He went to the Kerith Ravine east of the Jordan, and he stayed there. The ravens brought him bread and meat in the morning and bread and meat in the evening, and he drank from the brook. The ravens deliver breakfast and dinner and Elijah is nourished with water from the steadily receding stream. Elijah has embarked on an adventure of trust.

Here's a crucial question for the reader of the Elijah story: What if this journey of trust is not restricted to Old Testament prophets? What if God still whispers to his children, "Just do what I'm asking you to do. Go where I ask you to go, and stay where I ask you to stay, and I will provide for your daily needs. Look after my interests and I will look after you. Trust me."

Learning Trust

Thanks to the faithfulness of my parents in relaying stories of God's generosity from their own lives, the truth that God provides is something I absorbed in childhood. In their early days of ministry, when money was so scarce and God so good, they saw his gracious hand again and again. This reality became not simply part of my parents' story of faith but a foundational part of my story of faith. It was grafted into me.

As twenty-one-year-old newlyweds and in my final year of college, Chris and I were invited to serve at Ada Bible Church in Grand Rapids, Michigan, a ministry of a couple dozen people. I believe that I was handcrafted, tailor-made for the economic adventure that accompanied this start-up church. Witnessing God's faithfulness to my parents had prepared me for the journey of trust we were about to embrace.

But my background was radically different from that of my newlywed wife. Though "I" was ready, "we" were not ready. While I was raised in a pastor's family, Chris's father ran a successful insurance office. While I was raised in ministry, attending church every time the door was open, she attended sporadically, becoming a devoted Christian in late high school. While I had a legacy of stepping out in faith and seeing God provide what was needed, this adventure was totally new to her. Can you sense the breeze of conflict blowing as we entered marriage and ministry together? We had simply come from two different backgrounds, and I was far more prepared to embrace a life of routine financial shortage than she was.

Growing up in my family, there was a sense that even though things were tight financially, there somehow would always be enough. This sense was alien to Chris. Our conflict accelerated when I proposed that we begin the practice of tithing. Tithing is the life discipline of living on 90 percent of your income so that 10 percent can be given away. As we started our married life, as I served this small congregation while completing school, and as Chris worked as a minimum-wage receptionist, our combined income placed us below the poverty line. And here I was, suggesting that we commit to giving 10 percent of our income away.

When Chris balked, I felt the concept needed expounding: Tithing, I explained, means that when our annual income reached $16,000, we'd give $1,600 away. When our income reached $20,000, we would give $2,000 away. The challenge wasn't that Chris misunderstood the math; the challenge was that she thought this was crazy. How could we possibly give money away and still be capable of buying a house or putting gas in the car or buying groceries, for that matter. I was speaking an unintelligible language. I simply made no sense to her.

Now, I assure you the issue at stake was not that I was generous and that she was greedy. Our friends who know us well can testify that Chris has a far more generous spirit than I do. I am confident, also, that the difference between us was not that I was mature but she was immature. Trust me on this one, my capacity for immaturity was immense. What I believe we were dealing with was fear. Chris was scared, and her sense of dread was not irrational. Reason was on her side. Her fear was based in the real possibility that if we gave money away, we would not have enough for our basic needs. In fact, we really didn't have enough for our basic needs before we gave money away.

Understanding this distinction between greed and fear is crucial. Though greed can certainly stifle generosity, I believe the more frequent culprit is fear. The decisive question becomes, "If I give this away, what if I don't have enough for me?" Fear of not having enough can paralyze generosity. Fear wars with trust, each battling to become the dominant force in our decision making.

I credit Chris's growth in this area not to my powers of persuasion but to God's movement in her heart. With not a little apprehension, we began our life practice of systematic giving. Honestly, as I look back, I wonder how we made it. But though things were often strained financially, God proved his reliability again and again to us. In these early days of ministry, there was always food for the next meal, and somehow we always had a few dollars for gas to get where we needed to go.

I wish I could testify that our attitudes were always positive, but this would be less than truthful. On occasion we succumbed to self-pity and even resentment over our situation. But God's grace prevailed. We were following God's leading in our lives, and he was faithful to provide for our basic needs. Not all our wants. Not all we desired. But he faithfully met all of our needs. Borrowing from the farming imagery Paul used to encourage the Corinthians, we were faithful to scatter seed, and God was faithful to provide the harvest.

Our decision to honor God through systematic, percentage giving was as much about trust as it was about generosity. Looking back, we are so thankful that we took this leap of faith. This was one of our defining moments in the journey of trust, and we are grateful that it occurred early in our marriage.

That's a bit of our story. What does yours look like? I urge you to embrace giving as a lifestyle. Be decisive and act immediately before this critical movement gets procrastinated, postponed, and ultimately forgotten. This is a move you will never regret.

16

The Ongoing Challenge

The Concert

Ashley had looked forward to the concert for months. As she drove from her college apartment to the fine arts center, her intention was to see a great show, not to have her heart moved to sponsor an impoverished child. But during the intermission, as the musicians retreated backstage, a video played on the massive screens. "For just over a dollar a day," the narrator reasoned, "you can change the life of a child." Contrasting images unfolded during the five-minute pitch. Depressing scenes of slum children living in rags were interspersed with those of grade-schoolers clothed, nourished, and sitting at simple, wooden school desks. "For only $38 a month—just over a dollar a day—you can make a difference in the life of a child," the narrator repeated as the video drew to a close.

Numbed by overexposure to a parade of agencies seeking funding for one cause or another, Ashley considers herself immune to this sort of appeal. She is surprised that the intermission video moved her, but it clearly did. The rush of the second half of the show isn't enough to push the images of the school-aged children from her mind. "I know I waste more than a dollar a day," she confesses as she drives through the darkness back to her apartment. She reflects on the money that slips through her fingers without much thought or notice, money spent on the early morning mocha, midafternoon vending machine snacks, the clothes she buys but doesn't really need. "I could do this," she whispers out loud. "I'm going to do this," she resolves.

But then she does some quick calculating. Thirty-eight dollars a month over twelve months is over ... $450 a year! "That's ridiculous. I'm a college student, working a part-time job! I don't have that kind of money to give away!"

Her dilemma is pretty simple. If she commits to giving this money, how can she be assured there will be enough for her? Though this interior debate may seem trivial, it is a critical moment in Ashley's spiritual formation. Something vital is at war within this university senior as she ponders this opportunity and the accompanying cost. A twenty-two-year-old is invited into the journey of generous living. As she calculates the commitment of $38 a month, over $450 dollars a year, she is actually calculating whether or not God can be trusted. This moment of conflict is pivotal, because Ashley's response to this prompting could either unleash or stunt her growth as a disciple of the Christ.

Let's return to Elijah in the Kerith Ravine. Though his situation is extreme when contrasted to a college student wrestling over the gift of a bit more than a dollar a day, the underlying principle is the same: obedience requires trust.

The Widow's Bread

As the drought burns the land, the brook grows ever more shallow. I imagine the day when the water ceases to flow and Elijah quenches his thirst by seeking standing pools, then the search for random puddles, then ... then what? As the water disappears from the ravine, he has received no new direction. Did he ever feel like screaming to the sky, "Remember me!? I'm still down here! I'm down to my last puddles of water! What am I supposed to do now? Hello!? Is anybody up there listening?" At last, when all that remains of the gurgling stream is a ribbon of dry rock, the prophet receives new direction:

> Then the word of the LORD came to him: "Go at once to Zarephath in the region of Sidon and stay there. I have directed a widow there to supply you with food."
>
> (1 Kings 17:8–9)

Elijah's time of raven-catered breakfast is over. But does the new source of nutrition seem promising to you? A widow has been directed to feed Elijah. I suppose it is overly optimistic to suspect that this will be an affluent, well-heeled widow. Incidentally, this town, Zarephath, is in Phoenicia, the homeland of Queen Jezebel who is hunting Elijah down. Perhaps the last place she would suspect him to flee is to her own backyard.

Elijah embarks on a new phase of his journey, across the baked ground to Zarephath near the Mediterranean coast. Upon arriving, there by the town gate, he sees a widow gathering sticks. The prophet, parched from his journey, implores:

> "Would you bring me a little water in a jar so I may have a drink?" (1 Kings 17:10)

This seems a reasonable request. But as she heads off to draw some water, he adds, "And bring me, please, a piece of bread" (v. 11). This, in a time of famine, is probably not a reasonable request. In response, the widow turns toward Elijah and utters one of the most pathetic, wrenching confessions found in the Bible.

"As surely as the LORD your God lives," she replied, "I don't have any bread—only a handful of flour in a jar and a little olive oil in a jug. I am gathering a few sticks to take home and make a meal for myself and my son, that we may eat it—and die" (v. 12).

The resignation in her brief response is numbing. "I'm sorry. But you see, I'm gathering firewood for the last supper. I will collect these sticks and then return home to mix our flour with a little water and make a bit of dough. Then I will kindle the fire and bake our bread. Then my son and I will sit and dine together on bread and oil. And then we will proceed to starve to death."

This is the point in the story where we anticipate a profound and heartfelt apology. Elijah has obviously inconvenienced the wrong widow. But instead of an apology, he tells the woman not to be afraid. He instructs her to go home and do what she has described but to amend her plans slightly. She is to return home and bake bread for herself and her son. First, however, if it's not an imposition, she is to make some food for Elijah. The prophet then forecasts the impossible. The jar of flour will not run out and the jug of oil will not run dry until rain returns to the land. This shocking suggestion in the face of such utter desperation is either unbelievably cruel or unimaginably kind.

I'm expecting the impoverished woman to laugh bitterly, or scream, or curse this stranger. "What exactly do you take me for? Are you mocking my desperation? Making light of my death and that of my condemned son?!"

But she doesn't. We read, with economy of language, that, "She went away and did as Elijah had told her" (v. 15). Whoa, what's up with this? How could someone on the brink of starvation behave this way? A plausible answer is that she knew Elijah was coming. I suspect that she had advance notice. Remember back at the dry creek bed, before Elijah embarked on his journey the Lord informed him, "I *have directed* a widow there to supply you with food" (v. 9, emphasis added). Had this desperate woman been forewarned of Elijah's arrival? A man from Israel, a prophet, would arrive and ask for something outlandish, and she was to produce whatever he requested. I think the widow had been tipped off. Then, upon Elijah's arrival and outlandish request, she was forced to make a risky decision as to whether she would follow this bizarre directive.

The unnamed widow places her sticks on a bed of warm coals and fans them into a small fire. She portions out her powdered treasure — the flour, as precious as life itself. Water is blended in, dough is placed over the fire, and hospitality of the riskiest variety is offered. And the obedience of the destitute widow is seen by the God of heaven who delights in rewarding courageous faith.

> So there was food every day for Elijah and for the woman and her family. For the jar of flour was not used up and the jug of oil did not run dry, in keeping with the word of the LORD spoken by Elijah. (1 Kings 17:15–16)

Okay, we get the point: God uses the widow to feed Elijah. But there is something else here that is stunning. Remember that the widow and her son are about to starve. As the famine wreaks the land, not only does the widow feed Elijah, but through Elijah, God also feeds the widow. An insanely courageous act of obedience is honored by the God who loves to provide for those who strap in for the wild ride we call trust.

In the widow's story, trust prevails and God provides. It is a beautiful picture of God's care. But why is this story in our Bible? What are the implications for our lives? I suspect that our Lord is still calling us to trust him and longs for us to know how much he delights in our steps of faith. But trust is an ongoing challenge, a lengthy journey, and not something that is resolved with a single decision.

The Ongoing Challenge

As Chris and I progressed into our mid-thirties, our once tiny church was growing, and so was my salary. Then our youngest child, Alex, went off to school, and Chris began working part-time outside the home again. We were once more a two-income family. With increased financial stability we drove more reliable vehicles, we acquired new furniture, and we were now able to afford modest vacations. Though our financial lives were stabilizing, our progress felt sluggish compared with many of those around us. We felt as if we were driving in the financial "slow lane" while watching others speed past us.

As I reflect on that time, these differences in lifestyle between us and others may not have been totally income based. We had dedicated ourselves to the discipline of living on 90 percent of our income so that 10 percent could be given away. We also acquired a strong aversion to credit card debt, so were unwilling to buy things we could not immediately pay for. But our perception was that we were falling behind—or at least not surging ahead as rapidly as others.

We had largely moved past the season where there was fear of *not having enough*. I think this stage was more about the fear of *not being enough*. It was a season when we had to reconnect with our core spiritual identity and not a pseudo identity propped up by what we bought or owned.

These years were important for anchoring deep in our identity—remembering who we were—with or without the appearance of affluence. Our core identity was grounded in the reality that we were God's beloved son and daughter. The Creator of all the beauty that surrounds us had adopted us into his household and called us to enjoy him fully. This era of slow but steady financial growth was the time to remember again that I don't *get* my identity from my car. I *bring* my identity to my car. I don't get my identity from my house. I bring my identity to my house. I don't get my identity from my career. I bring my identity to my career. My identity is anchored in *who* I belong to, not *what* belongs to me.

There is a pool of wealth that is not money, and we were swimming in it.

My Precious Savings

I wish I could testify that the issue of trust was totally settled in my life. My experience is that the war doesn't end but simply takes on new shapes. The conflict does not evaporate but morphs into new forms and challenges.

Chris and I have now moved through our forties. Through the years, we dedicated ourselves to living more simply than we could afford to live. As our income rose, we resisted the impulse to embrace a larger mortgage simply because we could afford the payments. We elected to drive moderately priced vehicles to avoid car loans. We continue to studiously avoid credit card debt, purchasing things after we have saved up for them. These strategic steps have further increased our financial margin. The effect of this lifestyle is that we enjoy something we never had in the early years of marriage and ministry ... SAVINGS.

I love having savings. I love earning interest instead of paying it. I love watching it grow from month to month. I find the sensation of knowing I have a growing bank account thoroughly enjoyable. Okay, not merely enjoyable. I find a growing savings account intoxicating. Does anyone sense a new challenge brewing?

And here, I must confess, there are instances when I find it difficult to part with my precious savings when called upon to do so. Some time ago, our church was in another major building program (there have been several over the last thirty years). That December, I stood before our congregation and asked our people to consider giving a Christmas offering to offset the cost of our new facility. I invited our people to give a sacrificial gift that was above and beyond their normal giving. A short time after making this appeal to our people, I engaged in a brief wrestling match with God:

"And Jeff, what gift will you give this Christmas? You know that good leaders never ask their people to do what they are unwilling to do themselves."

"But I'm already giving 10 percent of my income to our church," I argued.

"Ah … but in your request you said, 'in addition to your regular giving.' That 10 percent is your regular giving. What will you give 'in addition' to that? And by the way … it better not be only a few hundred dollars."

"Why??? This is from my SAVINGS. My precious SAVINGS!" I whined.

"Because you asked your people to bring a *sacrificial gift* above their regular giving, and where you stand financially, a few hundred dollars is not a sacrifice."

"But it's my SAVINGS," I protested. "It's supposed to move forward and not backward!"

"And what is your savings for? What do you intend to do with it?"

"It's for stuff. Stuff out there in the future. You know,

like … what if I turn seventy-three and haven't put enough money away and may no longer work and earn an income!? What am I going to do then, huh? Who's supposed to take care of me then?"

Oops.

"Jeff, who took care of you when you were growing up? As your parents faithfully embarked in ministry, who intervened and lovingly answered their prayers? Who provided for them and for you in periods of shortage? Who met every need your family faced?"

"You did," I confessed.

"When you were starting out in ministry and were faithful to follow my leading to serve a small congregation, was there ever a time when your children went hungry or unclothed? Who took care of you then?"

"You did," I conceded. "And though things were tight, they never went hungry or lacked clothing. We always seemed to have what we truly needed and often enjoyed luxuries far beyond our basic needs."

"And in the years when you were gaining financial footing but feeling others were speeding past you, who provided the sense of belonging and identity to fill and sustain you?"

"You did," I confessed again.

"And now, in a time of financial stability and growth, who provides for you?"

"I do?" I offered.

"Let's try again. Who meets your needs now?"

"You do."

"Jeff, if I met your needs when you were a child, and if I provided for you in your twenties, if I have walked with you, and guided you, and given you strength when you were weak and wisdom when you were confused; if I have been faithful to this point, do you think you can trust me when you turn seventy-three? Can you trust me with your future?"

We wrote the check.

Never Out of the Woods

As I said, the war of trust and fear doesn't really end; it simply takes on new forms. If trust triumphs over fear in a season of scarcity, I can be assured that the two will duke it out again in a season of abundance. I am naive to believe that the final skirmish is behind me. I suspect that competition for my heart could be a lifelong battle. In the journey of trust, perhaps our greatest adventure lies ahead and not behind us.

The voice that whispered to Elijah and to the church in Corinth is alive and well. He calls us from our small worlds and invites us into an adventure of trust. Listen for his voice:

"Follow me and I will look after you. Just do what I'm asking you to do. Trust me in this adventure."

PART 5: The Generous Heart

Reflect and Discuss:

1. Do you agree that the enemy of generosity is often fear and/or a lack of trust and not stinginess? What do you think is the basis of fear and of lack of trust?

2. How can greater generosity lead us into greater contentment?

Project: Increase your giving by 1 percent for a month

Many of us get stuck. While seeing forward movement in paying off debt, paying down a mortgage, or increasing the percentage we invest, the percentage of our giving often gets stuck. For a month, increase your giving by 1 percent. If you currently give nothing away consistently, give away 1 percent of your earnings this next month. If you currently give 10 percent of your income away, boost this to 11 percent for a month. You get the picture.

Now ... here's the question. Is that new level sustainable? Is it possible that this should become a new practice?

PART 6

The Invitation

17

Back to the Beginning

The Anniversary

It's Friday evening. Ted and Brenda have invited dear friends to join them at their favorite Italian restaurant as they celebrate their twenty-fifth wedding anniversary. The evening is filled with great food and the kind of unencumbered laughter that accompanies close and enduring friendships.

As they dine on delicious pasta and warm bread, they reflect on their difficult start—marrying right out of college and working entry-level jobs to scrape by. They recall the days of filling an empty gas tank one quarter full and hoping to make it to the next paycheck before the tank ran dry, pillaging coins from the change jar, and returning bottles for the deposit to buy groceries. It seems like so long ago, and they have traveled such an unbelievable distance in two and a half decades. They now enjoy a successful business, a healthy marriage, and the benefits brought on by years of financial diligence. They worked hard, budgeted carefully, saved faithfully, and invested wisely. Now at the gas pump the tank is always filled, and they purchase groceries without penny-pinching drama.

Ted and Brenda are blessed. They have never been in a better place financially. They have never felt more economically secure. And they have never been in greater danger of spiritual drift. What makes their situation most tenuous is that they are utterly unaware that spiritual decay stalks the prosperous.

Here is a sobering thought: The spiritual disciplines that accelerate financial freedom may land you in a place where your spirit is in jeopardy. If you seek God's strength while refusing to play the comparison game, if you curb spending by declining purchases that cannot possibly fulfill you, and if you resist the magnetic pull of accumulating far more stuff than you need or could possibly use, there is a strong chance that you will become financially free. And financial freedom ushers in a whole new set of spiritual challenges.

This troubles me immensely. I wish a God-centered, financially disciplined life would irreversibly lead to a place where you are no longer in spiritual danger, but I find the opposite to be true. Here is the conundrum: If you are diligent, disciplined, and wise, there is a stronger possibility that your wealth will grow. If you work consistently, spend carefully, and avoid debt studiously, you have greatly increased your odds of tasting financial freedom. Now what? Now you have a growing bank account, which in turn can diminish your dependence on God. There is a strong possibility that the spiritual surrender that made wealth possible can lead us to a place where spiritual surrender no longer feels necessary.

Leaving the Desert

Let's explore two stories from the Bible that warn us about the spiritual decline that frequently shadows material blessing.

The first story finds us with the wandering Israelites. In Deuteronomy we witness an epic transition. After generations of slavery in Egypt and a forty-year detour in the desert, the people of Israel ready themselves to enter the land of promise. This move represents a massive upgrade to their lifestyle. They prepare to trade the wasting desert for brooks and streams and valley springs. As they ready to leave the land of scorpions and withering sun, they dream of agricultural abundance. Their future home has been called "the land flowing with milk and honey," a well-watered land where wheat, barley, grapes, figs, and pomegranates thrive. Olive oil flows as well as honey. They will have bread in abundance. The hills provide iron and copper waiting to be mined. The sons and daughters of Jacob prepare to thrive—they can nearly taste it. After a generation of desert living, their visions swell with sweet, sweet dreams of juicy grapes, fresh bread, tart pomegranates, and cool running water; a new land, a new home, and a new life. In a word, *prosperity*.

And here, east of the Jordan River, on the threshold of their mouthwatering transition, their faithful leader Moses offers a word of warning, a caution as they anticipate this monumental shift of fortune:

> When you have eaten and are satisfied, praise the LORD your God for the good land he has given you. *Be careful that you do not forget the LORD your God,* failing to observe his commands, his laws and his decrees that I am giving you this day. Otherwise,... when you build fine houses and settle down, and when your herds and flocks grow large and your silver and gold increase and all you have is multiplied, *then your heart will become proud and you will forget the LORD your God,* who brought you out of Egypt, out of the land of slavery.
>
> (Deuteronomy 8:10–14, emphasis added)

Their leader tells them simply, "When prosperity strikes, don't forget God." The reality we are confronted with in this story is that the blessing of wealth does not spontaneously result in growing devotion to God. In fact, the gravitational pull seems to be in the opposite direction. Unguarded, financial stability releases a slow slide of self-sufficiency that breeds independence from God. It is quite natural for the marriage of long hours, hard work, and smart decisions to result in the satisfied claim, "I did this. I earned this degree, I secured this job, and I slaved away for this promotion. I saved this money and bought this house and car and boat. I did this." The problem is that "I did this" glides imperceptibly into "I did this on my own. I did this without you." This was the dangerous trajectory the Israelites were on as they prepared to exchange the barren desert for fertile Canaan. Moses continues his warning:

> You may say to yourself, *"My power and the strength of my hands have produced this wealth for me."* But remember the LORD your God, for it is he who gives you the ability to produce wealth, and so confirms his covenant, which he swore to your ancestors, as it is today.
>
> (Deuteronomy 8:17–18, emphasis added)

Here we encounter the sobering reality that concerted effort is required to maintain spiritual devotion in the event of financial prosperity. As net worth climbs, a strong dose of self-awareness and humility are required if the heart is to move God-ward. I think of those haunting lyrics from the great hymn "Come Thou Fount of Every Blessing":

> "Prone to wander, Lord, I feel it.
> Prone to leave the God I love."

To preserve a humble heart before our Lord, our confession must continually be, "It is you, my God, who gives me the ability to produce wealth. You granted me a creative mind and have provided the opportunities I am now making the most of. I am working hard, but I comprehend that even my disciplined spirit is a gift from you. You have been with me, favored me, and your blessing has been with me. Please preserve my heart. As my situation improves, as wealth grows, as security compounds, may I not forget you. In my prosperity, please don't let me become an arrogant, thankless jerk."

The Bucket List

Now let's turn our attention to a second narrative that casts light on the spiritual drift that often accompanies growing wealth, and one man's deep longing to remain spiritually focused. Imbedded in the book of Proverbs we find a prayer attributed to a man named Agur. He asks God to grant him two wishes before he passes from this life.

> "Two things I ask of you, LORD;
>   do not refuse me before I die:
> Keep falsehood and lies far from me;
>   give me neither poverty nor riches,
>   but give me only my daily bread."
>
> (Proverbs 30:7-8)

What will Agur ask? What would you request? If you had two petitions of God before you die, what would they be? Opportunity? Travel? Popularity? Legacy? Adventure?

In the 2007 film *The Bucket List*, two men from radically

186

different backgrounds share a hospital room as they both battle terminal cancer. Carter (Morgan Freeman) is a mechanic, and Edward (Jack Nicholson) a crotchety multi-millionaire. As their friendship grows, they flee the cancer ward to spend their remaining weeks crossing off adventures from their bucket list—things they want to do before they "kick the bucket." The road trip takes them skydiving, climbing the great pyramids, and racing vintage cars. They chase the adventures they had often dreamed of but had never taken time to pursue.

So, how about you? Is anything on your bucket list? Anything you deeply long to do before your time on earth is over? Complete a marathon, stand beneath the Eiffel Tower, view the Grand Canyon, author a book, snorkel in the Caribbean, learn to make pasta, or visit the Great Wall of China? Is there anything you desire to see, learn, or achieve before you die? Remember the two things that seized Agur's heart—his bucket list prayer.

Request number 1: Honesty. "Keep falsehood and lies far from me." What a petition, what a longing. "Dear Lord, I deeply long to avoid deceit. I desire a life of integrity. Please guide my steps in such a way that I may not leave a trail of lies and a maze of deception in my wake." This is Agur's first request. He hungers for a life of honesty and begs God's help to prevent him from falling into a web of deceit.

Request number 2: Simplicity. "Give me neither poverty

nor riches, but give me only my daily bread." Now, this is not exactly what you would call the American prayer. Agur longs to land somewhere in the moderate middle. Not dirt poor. Not filthy rich. He asks only for daily provision to meet his daily need. Why in the world would anyone offer up such a prayer? What was this guy thinking?

As we explore Agur's reason behind this strange request, we meet a man who knows the darker corners of his own heart. He is keenly aware of his propensity to fall, to slide far from God. He asks for daily bread because:

> Otherwise, I may have too much and disown you
> and say, "Who is the LORD?"
> Or I may become poor and steal,
> and so dishonor the name of my God.
>
> (Proverbs 30:9)

This man knows his own heart. He suspects that a life of abundance may become a prelude to spiritual drift, actually disowning God. Agur also suspects that if he enters a season of severe shortage, he will not silently starve, but is certain that he will become a thief. Either extreme—affluence or poverty—may lead him to dishonor God. And so he prays, asking God to meet his daily needs in a way that will lead neither to a life of affluent spiritual drift nor dishonorable robbery.

As I reflect on Agur's bucket list prayer, I am struck by

the deep craving that lies behind the request. What this man desires most in life is to live in harmony with his God. Wealth is secondary. In fact, he recognizes that excessive wealth may prevent him from achieving his primary goal: that of walking with God and honoring God. He fears that abundance may lead to theological amnesia. As wealth grows, there is a subtle temptation to forget God.

Renewed Commitment

It's late when Ted and Brenda leave the delightful dinner, celebrating their first twenty-five years together. It was a delicious evening of food, friends, and laughter. As their headlights cut a path from the parking lot of the Italian restaurant and move toward home, they calculate what the next twenty-five years might bring. Out of a deep sense of gratitude for God's goodness in their lives, they pledge themselves to a simple prayer: "Lord, may we not forget you."

If the business continues to grow, may we not forget you.

With any prestige that may come with our success, may we not forget you.

As our savings increase, may we not forget you.

As we enjoy our house, may we not forget you.

We are where we are because of your goodness. Deliver us from the illusion that we did this alone, without your guidance and without your blessing. Lord, may we not forget you.

18

Rich Advice

Wedding Gifts

Chris and I married in Northern California in the summer of 1983. After our honeymoon, we loaded our green Ford Gran Torino and headed east on Interstate 80 for me to complete a final year of Bible college in Michigan. We had nothing really; just a few hundred dollars and a well-worn car with its trunk laden with our earthly possessions. Mainly the spoils from our wedding reception—blender, toaster, dishes, glasses, silverware, towels, and three or four cheese boards with domes, which apparently were a popular gift at the time.

Upon arriving in Michigan we landed minimum-wage jobs, and rented a small, one-bedroom, upstairs apartment that would be our home as I completed my studies. Thankfully, the apartment was furnished because we had no furniture other than a single bookshelf. Friends loaned us their extra TV. As I said, we started with nothing.

But pause for a moment and re-examine the "nothing" we had. Rewind the tape and carefully evaluate our scenario again. As a newlywed couple driving to Michigan we were wealthy educationally; we were literate and we were high school graduates. And why were we returning to Michigan? To complete a college education. The fact that we owned a car, even though it was older and a bit sketchy from a reliability standpoint, placed us among the world's affluent —something like only 10 percent of the globe's inhabitants possess an automobile. We had a trunk filled with new appliances that operated with consistent electricity pulsing through our apartment. And yes, the humble apartment. At age twenty-one we were capable of living independently of our parents. Add these benefits up: employed, educated, living independently, car owning, and possessing a trunk loaded with new household accoutrements. While we were just starting out and feeling profoundly below average, we were, by the standard of billions living in developing countries, unbelievably rich.

I'm not describing our abundance today as a solidly middle-aged and middle-class couple. This wealth was ours in the beginning, in the days when we were just starting out and had "nothing." Rich not only describes me now, with an emergency fund, reliable transportation, and home ownership. Rich describes us then, as twenty-one-year-old newlyweds moving into our first, small apartment.

How does Jesus intend to meet people like us, the world's financial elite whose daily anxieties do not revolve around

affording bread or securing basic clothing? As we live in affluence, to what felonies are our hearts susceptible? What guidance does the Scripture give to rich people—people such as
Chris and me as we made our way up the stairs of our first
apartment bearing boxes of wedding gifts?

Jesus Speaks to the Church

Chapters 2 and 3 in the book of Revelation contain letters
to seven churches in the Roman province of Asia (Western
Turkey). The significance of these seven messages intensifies
when we comprehend that they were spoken by the resurrected Christ. In our Bible, these letters comprise Jesus' last
message to his church. Congregations from seven communities hear words of affirmation and rebuke, warning, and
encouragement. The final group addressed is the congregation of Laodicea. Listen to this chilling reprimand spoken by
the risen Jesus.

> You say, "I am rich; I have acquired wealth and do not need
> a thing." But you do not realize that you are wretched,
> pitiful, poor, blind and naked. (Revelation 3:17)

This message describes a Jesus community that is financially self-sufficient yet spiritually bankrupt. For Christians
living in Laodicea, financial security had not translated
into spiritual vitality. Instead, their material prosperity had

resulted in poverty of the soul. As we dive deeply into their culture and story, we gain stunning insight into ours, and we are reminded that wealth often does not result in spiritual buoyancy.

The Wealth of Laodicea

Today, Laodicea is one of the most active archeological digs in Turkey. The unexcavated mound of only a few years ago is rapidly being unearthed to reveal a stunning main street with adjoining shops. Aged temple columns and residential homes emerge from centuries of being concealed beneath the soil. The outline of a major city comes to life hinting at the wealth that once belonged to Laodicea.

The city sat on the southern edge of the lush Lycus River Valley on a major east/west highway that ran between Syrian Antioch and Ephesus. It was a significant banking center and boasted a medical school famous for an eye salve called Phrygian powder. The textile industry prospered with the production of distinctive hooded cloaks made from the glossy black wool of lambs from the region.

Laodicea was financially prosperous and self-sufficient. In AD 60, when an earthquake devastated the region, Emperor Nero offered financial support to the cities wreaked by the disaster. But the Laodiceans declined imperial assistance. It seems to have been a "thanks, but we can take care of

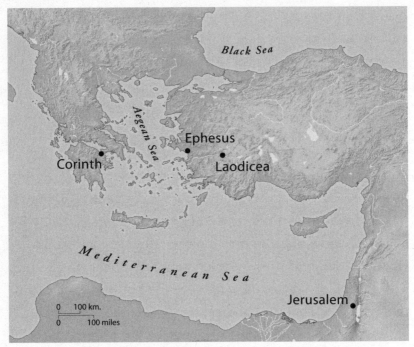

Laodicea in relation to Corinth and Ephesus.

ourselves" kind of refusal. They were the picture of self-sufficient affluence.

On occasions when I have visited the ruins of Laodicea, I have been struck with the impression that this would be an incredible place to live. In the United States, there are cities in regions with beautiful mountain views, while other regions are rich agriculturally; there are cities known for their financial markets, industry, and medical centers. In Laodicea, all these attributes came together in a single location. Not a bad place to call home. Standing by the ruins of the theater overlooking the rich valley below, I've thought, "I could live here."

But the beautiful location, ample food, and financial security had not drawn the Jesus community of Laodicea to devote themselves fully to their Lord. In fact, it appears that their affluence had numbed their hearts, unleashing significant spiritual drift.

What caused this spiritual decline in Laodicea? As we explore the messages to the other six churches in Revelation 2 and 3, we discover that they were menaced by a variety of hostile forces. Intense persecution, severe poverty, and false teaching threatened to overwhelm these other congregations.

In the message to the Laodiceans, however, there is no mention of crushing persecution, theological compromise, or financial hardship. Their greatest threat seems to be an arrogant self-sufficiency. They have become a wealthy church that no longer depends on God.

But in Christ's evaluation, they are destitute. Wretched. Pitiful. Poor. Blind. Naked. While they view themselves as capable and financially set, Jesus evaluates their condition as one of abject poverty. I find these words quite disconcerting. In Jesus' spiritual audit, he states, "*You do not realize* that you are wretched, pitiful, poor, blind and naked." The issue here is not simply the condition of spiritual poverty but that they were utterly unaware of their condition. What we witness here is flawed perception. They are in a desperate state and don't even realize it. The church had become spiritually fat, complacent, and shallow without knowing it.

Lukewarm

In his sober message to the church of Laodicea, Jesus employs the image of water temperature to describe their dulled spiritual condition.

> I know your deeds, that you are neither cold nor hot. I wish you were either one or the other! So, because you are lukewarm—neither hot nor cold—I am about to spit you out of my mouth. (Revelation 3:15–16)

Consider the metaphor with me. You're at a restaurant ready to order, and your server appears and asks, "What would you like to drink?" You respond with a request for tea. "Iced tea or hot tea?" she inquires. Both of these are respectable options. Soothing hot tea or refreshing iced tea. You, however, have something different in mind. "Do you have any tepid tea, something that has been sitting around for four or five hours? Neither soothing nor refreshing, neither hot nor cold, just somewhere in the pathetic middle?" Your server stands, pen in hand, in awkward silence.

This is how Jesus describes his sons and daughters whose hearts have been seduced by wealth. Who have no real need of him. Financially set. Spiritually pathetic. Lukewarm.

The physical setting of Laodicea adds currency to Jesus' indictment of lukewarm faith. Laodicea was one of three cities in this region of the Lycus River Valley. Colossae, ten miles to the east, was built beside a cold, running river. Hierapolis, six miles across the valley to the north, was renowned for its hot mineral baths. But Laodicea was dependent on a network of pipes to supply both hot and cold water to the city. Today, not far from the ruins of the stadium, a visitor can see an ancient water tower with clay pipes furred with sediment. One wonders how the water temperature was compromised due to its miles-long journey to the city. My suspicion is that the residents of Laodicea fully comprehended Jesus' image here. Lukewarm. Neither hot nor cold.

Would Christ describe you as lukewarm? Has your own abundance contributed to spiritual mediocrity? As possessions, savings, and sufficiency have grown for you, is your heart at risk of drifting? I think this is a serious question for the individual believer, but it has massive consequences for Christians as a collective group. I suspect that the greatest threat to authentic Christianity may be lukewarm Christianity.

As Jesus pleads with the Laodiceans, "I wish you were either one or the other" (hot or cold!), the resurrected Christ seems to be saying, "Please make up your mind. But don't dabble. Hot or cold, in or out. I did not come to give up my life, dying humbly on a cross, so you could dabble with amazing grace. Lukewarm Christianity is a threat to what I intend to do. It is the enemy of the hope I desire to bring, the life I intend to give."

Rich Advice

What counsel will Jesus give this affluent congregation? And how will our Lord advise those of us who are gaining the world but at risk of losing our souls? Listen to his encouragement.

> I counsel you to buy from me *gold* refined in the fire, so you can become rich; and *white clothes* to wear, so you can cover your shameful nakedness; and *salve* to put on your eyes, so you can see. (Revelation 3:18, emphasis added)

Gold, clothing, and eye salve. Do these items strike a familiar note? Do you remember what Laodicea was known for? To believers in a city renowned for its thriving banking system, rich black wool, and eye ointment, Jesus advises them to seek wealth from him (buy *from me* gold refined in the fire), to be clothed by him (white clothes to wear), and to have their spiritual blindness healed (salve to put on your eyes, so you can see). His message perfectly suited his audience, the imagery connecting powerfully with believers in Laodicea.

Through counseling them to seek his wealth, be clothed by him, and gain sight from him, Christ is imploring them—and us—to rely on his provision. He entreats us to recognize that there is a kind of wealth, covering, and healing that can

198

only be found in him. We must recognize how utterly lost we are without Christ. We need his presence, his favor, his blessing, his Spirit's power, every hour of every day. Walking with Jesus requires a confession that our affluence has limited power. As you read this, if you sense that prosperity has numbed your heart to God, there is hope. Jesus stands at the door and knocks.

19

Someone's at the Door

The Appearance of Christ

What does Jesus look like?

Close your eyes and picture the features of his face, his height, his hair. Are you aware of the influences that shape your perception of his appearance? I believe my personal image of Jesus was shaped by the artist Warner Sallman. Though you may be unfamiliar with his name, chances are your mental image of Jesus may also have been shaped by his art. In 1940, Sallman, a graduate of the Art Institute of Chicago, painted his now famous *Head of Christ*. Over the decades, this painting was reproduced into millions of prints that adorned churches, homes, and religious institutions. If your image of Jesus is that of a tall man with European features and long, gently flowing hair, then you have probably been influenced by Sallman's art.

Another popular Sallman painting revives a vivid childhood memory for me. In our small church, my pastor/father led Vacation Bible School each summer. Over the two weeks of "VBS," children accumulated points awarded for reciting memory verses or "coercing" friends to attend with them. These points could be exchanged for prizes arrayed on a table at the front of the sanctuary. The prizes ranged from pencils and balloons to more extravagant items for higher point totals. Among loftier items on the table were small mirrors, one with an image of Jesus knocking at a door.

Why a third-grade boy needed a handheld mirror is a mystery to me, but I remember amassing enough points to claim one as my own. The artist was Warner Sallman, and the picture of Jesus knocking is titled *Christ at Heart's Door*. Whenever I see the picture today, I flash back to my childhood church, the table of prizes, and the long-lost mirror.

Sallman's painting was inspired by Revelation 3:20 and its powerful image of Jesus at the door.

> Here I am! I stand at the door and knock. If anyone hears my voice and opens the door, I will come in and eat with that person, and they with me.

This verse is well known, but the context is often lost when the Scripture is recited. Jesus is standing at the door of the Laodicean church. To the church that had become financially self-sufficient yet spiritually bankrupt, he has come and he is knocking. He is calling. He waits for the door to open. Jesus wants in. His words are deeply stirring and inviting. "If anyone hears my voice and opens the door, I will come in and eat with that person, and they with me."

Jesus is offering friendship to those who have lost their way. He extends an open invitation to those who have become prosperous and spiritually dull. He asks them to open the door and dine. Dine with him. Are you ready for some good news? Jesus befriends materialists.

If you find yourself caught in the quest for endless accumulation, if you sense that your desire for a growing savings account has eclipsed your craving for the nearness of God, if you detect that wealth has numbed your spiritual sensitivity, be encouraged. There is hope. There is an invitation. Jesus knocks.

Dinner with Jesus

The image of Jesus inviting himself in for dinner is powerful, but it is even more stirring when we explore his invitation through a first-century lens. Recall an interaction that occurred near the beginning of Jesus' public ministry. He is near Capernaum on the northern edge of the Sea of Galilee. Passing a tax collection booth, he sees Matthew and invites him to become a devoted learner, a disciple. That Jesus would choose a tax collector as a close associate is something of a scandal. The Romans, who controlled Galilee, sold taxation rights to Jews, who in turn taxed their fellow countrymen—

their neighbors. During this time period, many of the bloody uprisings against Rome originated as tax revolts. Needless to say, tax gatherers were seen as traitors and bitterly hated.

And Jesus invites a tax gatherer to become a disciple—a close associate, a friend. Matthew leaves his collection booth and accepts the invitation to follow. That evening, Matthew hosts a dinner with Jesus as the guest of honor and invites his tax collector friends to the feast. I picture this dinner as a kind of going away party that Matthew throws for himself.

Look into the open courtyard and watch them eat, talk, and laugh. It looks like a tax collectors convention, with Jesus in the middle of the mix. Look also at the stunned, baffled reaction of puzzled onlookers. The Scripture records:

> While Jesus was having dinner at Matthew's house, many tax collectors and sinners came and ate with him and his disciples. When the Pharisees saw this, they asked his disciples, "Why does your teacher eat with tax collectors and sinners?"
>
> (Matthew 9:10–11)

What's going on here? Why the disdain over Jesus' dining companions?

In Western culture, we most frequently eat food that sits on a plate in front of us. It is *my* food on *my* plate. But in first-century Israel, as in many mideastern cultures today, bread was dipped into common bowls containing various blends of herbs, oils, and condiments. When you ate with someone, you ate *with* someone. The close proximity and common bowls in the dining experience expressed friendship in a way that is far different from a casual business lunch today. In their culture, to share a meal was to share a life. Dining was an invitation into friendship.

Thus the outrage of the Pharisees at the sight of Jesus dipping bread with Matthew's friends. The mingling of Jesus with the tax gatherers is scandalous. The Pharisees express their offended confusion to Jesus' disciples: "Why does your teacher eat with tax collectors and sinners? They cripple us financially. The tax gatherers collude with Rome and betray our people. How can your teacher dip his bread into a common bowl with them? How can he possibly extend friendship to *those* people?"

Overhearing the inquisition, Jesus responds: "It is not the healthy who need a doctor, but the sick" (v. 12). He offers a medical parable as his answer. Who seeks medical treatment? It is those who realize there is a real problem that needs curing, who seek out a doctor's help. This is how Jesus earned the title "the Great Physician." That term of honor comes from this story, where Jesus likens himself to a doctor.

The same Jesus who dined with Matthew and his friends knocks and calls to the Laodicean believers who have become financially affluent but spiritually bankrupt. He asks to come inside and dine. He extends an offer to eat with them, and with this, an offer of friendship, companionship.

Here I am! I stand at the door and knock. If anyone hears my voice and opens the door, I will come in and eat with that person, and they with me.

What an unbelievable invitation to me, to us. He's knocking.

To those with full closets but empty hearts. He's knocking.

To those who shop to cure loneliness or boredom. To those amassing wealth at the cost of generosity. To those whose wallets have become their god. He's knocking.

To those plagued with credit card debt through the undisciplined habit of spending more than they earn. To those plagued with envy. He's knocking.

To those with beautiful homes who feel inadequate when they compare themselves to those with even more beautiful homes. He's knocking.

He stands. He knocks. He calls. To Matthew and to wealthy believers in Laodicea—and to us. He wants in. He whispers, "Find spiritual wealth, clothe yourself in me, be healed from the blindness that obstructs true vision. Here I am. I stand at your door and knock." It is an invitation to the church that has lost its way. It is an invitation to me. It is an invitation to you. It's time to open the door.

PART 6: The Invitation

Reflect and Discuss:

1. How does contentment assist us in fighting against self-sufficient pride and lukewarm faith?

2. What does it mean to you that Jesus wants fellowship with us (Rev. 3:20)? How can his offer transform our lives and bring about contentment?

Project: Choose a transforming next step

It is likely that something has seized you over the last six weeks. What practice or discipline should be continued?

- Perhaps you are continuing to identify items around your house that are never used by you but could be used by someone else. It might give you great delight and be good for your spirit to give these items away. The Lord will be pleased to bring people to mind who might need things that are piling up around us.

- Continue the shopping fast. Many of you found this a soul-cleansing experience to simply enjoy the things you own without needing the "fix" of buying something new. Consider continuing the spending fast for another week or even longer.

- Jump another percentage in giving. Some of you have been stuck at the same level of giving for years, and the exercise of raising your giving a percentage point was freeing and liberating. There is a liberation that comes with giving. You may decide to immediately jump another percentage point.

- Serve faithfully. Serving frees us to think of others. Rather than serving "here and there, from time to time," commit to faithfully serving—week in and week out. Commit yourself to visiting weekly at a veterans facility, becoming a children's Sunday school teacher, or participating in a ministry of calling on the sick or those who are shut in. Humble, faithful serving liberates us from a self-absorbed life.

So, where do we go from here? It is important to decisively and immediately take a radical next step if you desire to continue to move toward the satisfied life.

Conclusion

On a beautiful spring day, Chris and I enjoy a Friday walk through an older neighborhood near downtown Grand Rapids. From time to time we stroll in this area wondering what it would be like to exchange our rural home for urban living where restaurants and coffee shops are within walking distance. We love the city and could imagine ourselves at home in a more pedestrian lifestyle.

We pass a brick house with a For Sale sign and pause for a moment to read the flier itemizing the square footage, number of bedrooms and bathrooms, and of course, the cost. As we walk, we begin yet another round in an ongoing conversation—to move or not to move. We live in the house in which we raised our children, a home that is more than adequate, and yet we find ourselves nosing around from time to time wondering if a move lies somewhere out there in our future.

Our conversation is marked by an overarching tone of freedom. We feel free to stay and free to move. Whatever we decided, we are confident of a few things:

- If we are incapable of finding contentment in our

current home, most assuredly we will not find contentment in a new one.

- A different house cannot define us, rescue us, or fill us. Any latent emptiness or dysfunction will stalk us to a new dwelling. And our real identity and fullness will follow us as well. Who we are, foundationally, cannot be altered with a new address.

- We are deeply committed to a lifestyle that includes serving and sharing. Therefore, we will not allow the choice of a home to erase financial margin and cripple giving. The amount we are willing to pay for a different house will affirm that the kingdom we are building is not our own.

- The crowning achievement in any home is the laughter and life enjoyed there. We trust that any dwelling we choose or remain in will be a haven for family and an oasis to friends and strangers.

My sincere hope is that as I continue to grow and mature, people will increasingly know me as someone who lives the contented, satisfied life.

May this also be true of you.

Acknowledgments

To my wife, Chris, with whom I have shared the journey toward the satisfied life. Thanks, babe, for your encouragement, love, and patience through another book project.

I am deeply grateful to the Zondervan team whose hard work and dedication made *Satisfied* possible. Special gratitude goes to Carolyn McCready. Carolyn, thank you for believing in this project from the beginning and guiding me through the writing process. I also want to thank Jim Ruark and Jean Bloom for their outstanding editorial assistance and Kim Tanner for her help with the maps. Much appreciation to Alicia Mey, Chris Fann, and John Raymond for their help and guidance along the way.

My appreciation to Wolgemuth and Associates — Erik, Andrew, and Robert: thanks huge. Erik, I am deeply indebted to you for our conversations about the satisfied life and your interest in the project from day one. Your Denver small groups who test-drove the material provided insight and encouragement. Thanks.

Major thanks to Marsha Sweet, my thoughtful ministry

assistant, who works tirelessly to help keep the various aspects of my ministry life together.

My deep gratitude to dear friends Meg and Kevin Cusack. Your friendship and love have upheld us. Your example in honoring God with your finances has inspired us. Meg, thanks for raking over the manuscript and offering guidance.

Special thanks to a special group: Ben and Laura, Steve and Jen, Rich and Ash, Brad and Laura, Jill and Ryan, and Jay and Darcie. Our time together was life giving.

Finally, I wish to express my appreciation to the congregation of Ada Bible Church, where many of these concepts were first developed in sermon form. Your open and receptive hearts make ministry a delight.

Satisfied Study Guide with DVD

Discovering Contentment in a World of Consumption

Jeff Manion
with Christine M. Anderson

Why is a contented, satisfied life so eva-sive? What deep hungers drive the reckless purchasing habits, out-of-control accumulation, and crazy consumer lifestyle for so many of us? And why are we often driven more by what our neighbors own than what will truly make us happy?

In this DVD-based Bible study, popular communicator and pastor Jeff Manion provides an inspiring and transformative vision for living a deeply contented life in the midst of our consumer-driven, materialistic, and often shallow culture. In light of our surroundings, Manion asks a critical question: Is it possible to live a deeply satisfied life, one of great inner joy, even as dreams seem to fade?

Satisfied draws richly from seven passages of Scripture, exploring the way in which these messages were received by the original readers and how these passages can alter the way we view wealth, accumulation, and ultimate contentment today.

This study guide contains video notes, individual or group reflection questions, and between-session personal projects enhancing your journey through each of the video sessions on the enclosed DVD, taught by Jeff Manion.

Available in stores and online!

ZONDERVAN®
.com

The Land Between

Finding God in Difficult Transitions

Jeff Manion

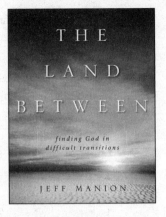

Author Jeff Manion uses the biblical story of the Israelites' journey through the Sinai desert as a metaphor for being in an undesired time of transition. After enduring generations of slavery in Egypt, the descendants of Jacob travel through the desert (the land between) toward their new home in Canaan. They crave the food of their former home in Egypt and despise their present environment. They are unable to go back and are incapable of moving forward. Their reactions provide insight and guidance on how to respond to God during our own seasons of difficult transition.

The Land Between provides fresh biblical insight for people traveling through undesired and difficult transitions such as foreclosure, unemployment, uncertainty, and failure. Such times provide our greatest opportunity for spiritual growth. God desires to meet us in our chaos and emotional upheaval, and he intends for us to encounter his goodness and provision, his hope and guidance.

The Land Between: A DVD Study

Finding God in Difficult Transitions

Jeff Manion

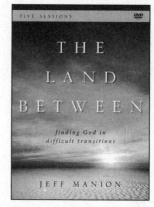

In *The Land Between*, pastor Jeff Manion uses the biblical story of the Israelites' journey through the Sinai desert as a metaphor for being in an undesired time of transition. After enduring generations of slavery in Egypt, the descendants of Jacob travel through the desert (the land between) toward their new home in Canaan. They are unable to go back and are incapable of moving forward. Their reactions provide insight and guidance on how to respond to God during our own seasons of difficult transition.

The Land Between is a five-session small group Bible study providing fresh biblical insight and hope, guidance, and encouragement for people traveling through undesired and difficult transitions — foreclosure, unemployment, uncertainty, and failure. Such times provide our greatest opportunity for spiritual growth. God desires to meet us in our chaos and emotional upheaval, and he intends for us to encounter his goodness and provision, his hope and guidance.

In *The Land Between*, you will learn:

- How to respond to God during your times of transition and difficulty
- How to find God in your pain and trust him in your waiting
- That the land between is essential for faith transformation and growth

Available in stores and online!